A SOLDIER'S DIARY
OF THE
GREAT WAR

A SOLDIER'S DIARY
OF THE
GREAT WAR

*

WITH AN
INTRODUCTION
BY

HENRY
WILLIAMSON

LONDON
FABER & GWYER
24 RUSSELL SQUARE

FIRST PUBLISHED IN MCMXXIX
BY FABER & GWYER LIMITED
24 RUSSELL SQUARE LONDON W.C.I
SECOND IMPRESSION APRIL MCMXXIX

CONTENTS

INTRODUCTION BY HENRY WILLIAMSON *page* vii

A SOLDIER'S DIARY OF THE GREAT WAR 3

1914 3

1915 85

1916 147

1917 207

EPIGRAPH 249

INTRODUCTION

BY
HENRY WILLIAMSON

READING this Diary now, years afterwards, it appears to me to have, within
its scope, a definite historical interest. Not
history as it is known to many school children;
there is little in it 'about deeds or lands, nor
anything about glory, honour, dominion, or
power'. A little, yes—the reader must find
for himself the passage where the young
cadet, having experienced war, forgets the
reality of that experience when listening to a
lecture on the retreat from Mons. His
imagination is excited by the 'great story'
of the gunners who 'worked like heroes'.
Whereas a few months before he had seen
those men, or their like, coming out of the
battle which lit the nights of Flanders at the
end of that retreat.

Saw some stragglers from the lines come limping in,
incredibly dirty and played out. They had a fortnight's

growth of beard, were plastered with mud from head to foot, greatcoats ragged and torn, some without arms, all barely able to drag one foot after another. They were hobbling back in small groups or singly—quite a small number in all. Wonder who and what they are, remnants of a defeated battalion, or stragglers that have lost their units, and are making their own way back? We gazed at them in wonder and pity; hope we never come to look like that.

That is an authentic entry, direct from actuality; whereas the excitation of the young man listening, in more or less comfortable conditions in the Divisional School in the Rue de Musée, Bailleul, to the military lecture, is derivative from a mental attitude ready-made and, alas! (remembering those four years) the commonplace of Europe. Terms glorifying deeds of infamy were— and are still—usual; and until those deeds are seen plain, as monstrous impositions on the young by the old, and the terms and memorials glorifying them are generally regarded with scorn for that they are lies about other people, the infamy will remain concealed, and will periodically renew itself.

The Diary was written during the War, and is, within its limits, true. It is limited in that it omits much that the Diarist, writing

in good weather in the front line when there
was 'nothing doing', or in billet or back-
area hut, either considered unwritable or
'not the sort of thing that should be written'.
There are innumerable other reasons for
these limitations, which can be summed up
in the simple statement that the Diarist was
not the man that he is now. The entries
are personal, yet seldom subjective; usually
vivid, and always restrained. They are the
writings of a man who seeks, within his little
book, that privacy and self-communion which
in the land of his birth would be unexpressed,
part of his normal life.

He was not greatly unhappy; there are no
wild outpourings in the Diary, no cries of
despair, even towards the end when the
haunted flying-man forces himself to take
cross-country runs in order to keep himself
fit for his work. The book reveals a man
sensitive and without hate, one not too intro-
spective, yet imaginative enough to know
what others are feeling, one who held himself
in discipline that his foremost duty should be
to his subordinates; a man who never shirked
what he was told to do, and yet sometimes,
because of his regard for those subordinates,

made protest—the best type of civilized man, and one of the best types of soldier. (Qualification is necessary for exactness, for there were other good types of soldier; and the very traits which made their excellence on the battlefield were not always esteemed in civil life.)

To many these pages will appear entirely true; to almost as many they will be typical of the War as the ordinary man saw it. It is unnatural to set oneself to recreate periods of great distress. We call such creations works of genius when they are made; such is *Le Feu*, by Barbusse. Our Diarist merely records the outlines of events and personal details for his own private satisfaction, and the many who served in the Army will find in this day-by-day human history jumping-off points from which their memories will go forward again into old activities. This soldier of the Great War, at odd moments during four and a quarter years of his life, set down —secretly, sometimes furtively, for diaries were forbidden by General Routine Orders —the salient features of his immediate past as they unconsciously arose in his mind, and never with the idea of other eyes reading

what he wrote.   He made his entries without
idea of any 'public', without a conscious
sense of composing and arranging his material.
Perhaps for that very reason of spontaneity
his narrative is so balanced, so vivid, so simple,
so readable.

   These dozen and more years afterwards,
it is interesting for a stranger (we are all
strangers when we look back on our pasts)
to consider the effect of war experience upon
a youthful consciousness; to discern how
vividness and sense of actuality grow with
nervous attrition, until, at the end of the
Diary, the War—that is, the contributing
human acts, a few of which in 1915 helped
to make a 'great story'—is seen plain, as an
'awful blind waste and brutality'.   The
stranger looks with clear sight into the past,
and sees again what the Diarist of 1914–1918
did not, could not, write.   Truth is relative:
the diary is truthful, and yet not truthful as
the stranger, sitting by the fire, recalls that
fled reality.   The young soldier of 1914
wrote:

   Last night we floundered out through an ice-bound
slippery communication trench to the reserve line in the
wood.   Water in our water-bottles was frozen by the

morning, but by lying close we kept fairly warm; had
some straw. Quite a picnic; not so cramped here.

The stranger by the home fire sighs, and
says to himself, is that all? A picnic? For
life in the reserve line in Ploegsteert Wood
on that night meant crawling and being
pulled, out of trenches filled with icy water to
the lousy crutch of the trousers: overburdened
men in mud-slabbed overcoats staggering
slowly into the wood, to lie down in low shelters
of hewn green oak-branches with roofs of mud-
filled sandbags, sharp and brittle with brown
icicles. Christ! it was cold . . . the boots
froze stiff, and glittered with frost, while a
chaos of shadows ceaselessly fled in the
leafless trees, shadows bent and vanishing in
the pallid light of flares sinking beyond the
eastern edge of the wood. Bullets cracked
among the tree-tops, and thudded into the
earth-mounded shelters; or, arising in richo-
chet into the sky, fell with sounds strangely
plaintive, between a buzzing and a whining,
into the marshes of the wood. The sounds
of the spent bullets falling—the wavering
greenish pallor of the flares and the silent
crooked rising shadows of trees—the swinging
of charcoal fires in ration tins perforated by

bayonet-jabs—the drone of stray German shells and the red-smoky crash and rattle of shrapnel—perhaps four white stabbing flashes and screaming *paa-aa-angs* of our field guns farther back in the wood—sudden startling *crack crack crack* of a machine gun traversing and snapping branches—slow shuffling movements of feet and toneless oaths of a ration party passing by; an eighteen-inch cube glinting shoulder-high, tin box with hard biscuits that made indifferent fuel in the buckets—'My Gawd, this is what we volunteered for! Talk about swinging the dripping on the troops!' greeted with grimly joking remarks—the slow and sombrous plodding past of stretcher-bearers greeted with silence—the whirr and grating cry of a bewildered pheasant—in the morning more half-hundred-weight boxes of bully beef, tobacco, biscuits, cast away unwanted among the splintered trees, and in shell-holes glazed with grey-green ice—mittened hands swung and thumped against stiff and creaking greatcoats—frost pushing its thorns into the quick of each nail on fingers and toes— rumours of the battalion going home after Christmas, 'coming from the latrine, as usual!'

—bitter agony of frost-bite, yet welcome, for thaw meant the chill of mud which absorbs your very life, your life enslaved and horizonless.

These were the sensuous impressions of 'ordinary' life in the reserve line of the wood at night, which all felt in varying degrees. A few realized the new life poignantly; to them the wood was desolate and sad, a living tomb haunted by the wandering spirits of the life of lost things, gone for ever. To others, it was at first enjoyable (before the mud deepened to the knees), a natural life after routine clerical work in a London office; a life hard but endurable, affirmed by comradeship. To most it was a thing for which they had committed themselves, and which they would 'stick'—indeed, there was no alternative, except by way of wounds or death. Later, many hoped for disabling wounds; but regimental history does not record these aspirations.

And yet (for suffering is relative) there came a time, not many months afterwards, when those men looked back on the Plugstreet life as one of ease and peace. That was just after the Division went into its first

rest since the Retreat.   After a few days the
order was given to be prepared to move at an
hour's notice; the eastern sky quivered and
blazed with light, and long and heavy rever-
berations rolled down the wind.   The battalion entrained, and after a night near
Poperinghe marched along a straight elm-set
road towards what was once a town, but now
a place of ragged hollow brick rectangles
and lath-and-plaster, a stone and mortar
waste that smoked, strewn with dead horses
and mules and men uncollected and unlimed.
Salvoes of 17-inch shells filled the twilit air
with their brutal and torpid downward dron-
ing: vast ruddy fans opened on the immediate
horizon, glaring and darkening with smoke
which spread and drifted slowly long moments
after the upflung tons of masonry had dropped.
Then the stupendous *WOMP! WOMP!
WOMP! WOMP!* that made the breathing
of each waiting watching man very audible
to himself.   Hobbling files of men, with
faces pale as toadstools, moved past them,
some crouching as they leaned against the
trees, or slipping down limp and shuddering
and croaking with their mouths in the grass.
Our men marched on, into that great horizon

horseshoe everlastingly forged by gun-fire, encircled by everlasting white flares which interweave and cross in their rising, and hang still, and waver wanly as they sink slowly down, and leave, with their final ground hissing, an unutterably blasted darkness before the eyes staring out of trenches pounded and flattened, blackened and stinking afresh after each stupendously linked series of bright shell-blasts; until the senses fuse into a glassy delirium of unreality, and life, death, hunger, thirst, alike vanish.

Many had their disabling wounds during those days, but some were more than 'Blighty ones'; and of those left behind, their friends, slouching away from the horseshoe of fire and corruption—one hundred and eighty souls out of the thousand that had cheered when leaving Southampton six months before—did not want to speak. The newspaper accounts used the same old terms of glorification, but the eyes of the survivors, in their solitary moments, were vacant and haunted.

Even the best war-correspondent accounts are lies, like most regimental histories, in that they do not record all the truth. Compilations of military facts do not recreate the past; the rendering of reality is a titanic labour, and Titans are not usually followers of a tradition. (If they are war-correspondents they are soon out of a job.) With scarce exceptions the more glorious a military accomplishment appears in the imagination of the inexperienced, the more terrible was the actual experience. This does not include personal exploits, which often were exhilarating and enviable (and not seldom were carried out in an extremely spirited state—like that of the man in the trenches at Armentières who had to be forcibly restrained from going over the top against 'the whole bleeding Allemand Army'; and who, heroic exaltation having lapsed into unconsciousness, was hastily laid on a stretcher by his pals and covered with a blanket when the General was reported to be going round the trenches. 'Your Corps Commander salutes his glorious dead!' and the General passed on. Very soon the story had travelled throughout the whole British Expeditionary Force, with the gleeful explanation, 'And the fellow was tight on rum he'd won from the company sergeant-major's cubby-hole!').

The General of whom that story was told

B

commanded the brigade that held Ploegsteert Wood in 1914, and launched the attack
on German House and the sector of line
opposite the notoriously enfiladed Hampshire
T trench. I happened to be present when
the plan of attack was being discussed, and
the General explained an idea of his about
certain men carrying wire-netting mattresses
stuffed with straw which, being flung over
the enemy entanglements, would enable the
attackers to get rapidly into the enemy
trenches. The attack was made in daylight;
the survivors were blasphemous about it.
However, as the Diary records, in the entry
of December 22 made in the stable billet of
a brewery in Armentières, a Brigade Order
was issued afterwards to explain that the
attack was 'supposed to pin German troops
to this front, to prevent them fighting the
Russians'.

Does History record how many enemy
corps headquarters had their movement orders
cancelled owing to this floundering across
root-fields, lumpy with dead cows and men,
by a few hundred men yelling hoarsely in
their fear? On Christmas Day a friendly
soldier of the 133rd Saxon Regiment told

me that two Germans had been killed, and five wounded, in our attack . . .

But a stranger must not tamper with a Diary of war-time vintage; other wine, trodden from the fruit of that period, matures in different bottles. Here is the Diary, just as it was written except that certain names have been altered or deleted, and a slight re-arrangement of the material made for the reader's ease. Many, like myself, will wish that more of it had been written during those unrealizable days. Does the reader wish to know more about the author than the reticent and anonymous Diarist allows? He is to be seen at a certain reunion dinner held at the Connaught Rooms in London one night in the first week of November every year. Dark hair, beginning to grow grey above the ears; dark eyes, brilliant and sharp, in a pale, reserved face—the figure of a man sitting quietly, like one awaiting friendship, among noisier and less thought-ful 'old comrades'. Thrice smashed up in the War, once nearly mortally; and nearly killed again near Horley in Surrey during the Peace, when a touring car at 40 miles an hour hit and carried him thirty yards.

Happily married, with a small but jolly family. More I will not say about him, except that he will probably reappear one day, as he was in 1914, in another book or books.

HENRY WILLIAMSON

28 *December*, 1928.
Devon.

1914

1914

THE regiment was in annual camp at Eastbourne, but as I was suffering from synovitis of the knee, I was in Seaford on leave. The news in the papers looked so serious today that I could stand the uncertainty no longer, and decided to go to Eastbourne and see what was happening. I hobbled to Seaford station, but on reaching Eastbourne I discovered that the regiment had come down the day before as planned, but had been immediately sent back to London. Forthwith I took the first train to town and appeared that evening at Head-quarters. I met many fellows I knew there, hanging about all on edge with suppressed excitement, or at any rate, I was. The one topic is—'Are we coming in?' It will be a black shame if we do not stand by our friends. It appears that the mobilization orders are all written out, and waiting for the word.

August 4th.

Went to Benetfink's in Cheapside to buy a jack-knife, and a few other necessary articles for mobilization, and found the shop besieged with others doing the same.

August 5th.

The green envelope containing the mobilization order has arrived. In my eagerness and haste I tore the envelope badly, which is a pity, as it will make a good souvenir. It is marked :

ON HIS MAJESTY'S SERVICE.   URGENT.

MOBILIZATION.

Inside was a buff form—Army Form E 635, which is as follows :

TERRITORIAL FORCE.

EMBODIMENT.

NOTICE TO JOIN.

No., Rank
and Name. ....

London Regt. or Corps.

Whereas the Army Council, in pursuance

of His Majesty's Proclamation, have directed
that the *London Regt.* be embodied on the
5th day of *August* 1914,

You are hereby required to attend at *The
Row* not later than *8.15* o'clock that day.
Should you not present yourself as ordered
you will be liable to be proceeded against.

.............................*Adjutant.*

Date *4 Aug. 1914.*

With the embodiment notice were Battalion
Orders on Mobilization.

We had to be at Head-quarters at 8.15
today, and all day long Head-quarters has
been a busy hive of orderly confusion, khaki-
clad men pouring in with kit, and lining up
for medical inspection by the M.O. The
entrance has been blocked with men eager to
join up, so we shall be able to pick and choose
our recruits, and be up to full strength at
last. Our company parades to have our
sword-bayonets sharpened the day after tomorrow.

Owing to my lame leg I was turned down
by the doctor, and instructed to report again
in a fortnight, so home I went after this

eventful day. Though tired, it was some time before I felt like sleep. We are soldiers now, real soldiers; how long will it last? shall we go to France? What will they do with us if we ever get there? Above all, how and when can I get fit?

August 15th.

Went for a long country walk today to try out my leg. It held up for 17 miles, so I shall rejoin on Monday.

I have been to a blind masseur, who has sweated over my leg for 3 hours a day. I don't know who was more tired, he or I; but he has put me right.

I went over to Woolwich one day this week to have a look round. A busy scene on the Common, horses being brought in, guns, gun-teams, gunners everywhere; and all over the parched grass squads of men in civilian clothes being drilled by N.C.O.'s in khaki, in the dust and sunshine.

By the way, we had instructions in mobilization to bring with us the following:

1 pair socks in pocket of greatcoat.
Toothbrush.
1 pair bootlaces.
Towel and soap.
Razor and case.
Shaving-brush.
Table-knife, spoon, and
  fork.   ⎫In haversack.
Comb.
Housewife fitted with
  needles, thread, buttons,
  etc.
Clasp-knife with tin-open-
  er carried on person.

And we are going to get £5 10s. equipment money.

We also had to bring kit-bags with spare uniform, shirt, towel, and underclothing.

August 17th, Monday.
Rejoined the Regiment.

Yesterday I went down to Eastbourne for the day to say good-bye to my people who were staying at a boarding-house there. At lunch a bounder of a man cheerfully asked me if I did not think the war would be over

in a few weeks, with the Germans beaten?
Ass! Why doesn't he help?

Six companies (we still adhere to the eight-
company system) are quartered at some
school buildings in the City.   We are paid 1s.
a day, with 2s. in lieu of rations, and we are
allowed out to get our meals.   Buses are free
to soldiers in uniform.

Jarvis-Lloyd and Hinton, a corporal and
private in the company, have been out with a
vet. in a taxi commandeering horses.   Very
few of us know anything about horses (those
two are amateur yachtsmen) and in a crowd
like ours there are no volunteers for the jobs
of cook, boot-maker, or officer's batman.
Each morning we have a swim in the Public
Baths at Shoreditch.

August 19*th.*

Section, company, rifle, and Swedish drill
all day.   We feel real soldiers now; the free-
and-easy peace-time atmosphere is gone.

August 20*th.*

Réveillé at 5 a.m., and the regiment set off
on the march at 7, after coffee and biscuits.
As we tramped over London Bridge we met

the early morning crowds going to work.
They stopped and lined the pavements,
staring at us curiously. Many cheered, and
waved their hats. We marched by Ken-
nington, over Clapham Common, and through
Wandsworth to the rendezvous of all four
battalions in the brigade—the windmill on
Wimbledon Common. 'Daddy' Trott's wife
walked beside him every step of the way, an
act of devotion which caused much quiet
amusement in the ranks of the company.
When you come to think of it, I suppose it
is rough on married men, but most of us
would find our womenfolk an embarrassment
just now. I don't think his wife quite
realizes what we are in for, or does she realize
too well?

It is now 5.25 p.m., and we have not yet
had a meal today; we have just kept going on
odd biscuits from our haversacks. Some of
us are billeted in a school at Wimbledon.
We are packed pretty tight, which is lucky,
as we are to sleep on the bare boards, and
there are no blankets. We were halted all the
afternoon on Wimbledon Common, no doubt
while billets were being found. We have
managed to get a wash, and were allowed out

to forage for ourselves, so five of us went to
Clapham Junction, and had our long-delayed
meal at Sam Isaacs' restaurant.

August 22nd, Saturday.

Yesterday we marched, a sultry tramp, to
Hersham, by a rather devious route, arriving
about two o'clock. We have to carry our
own rations and all necessaries, as well as the
entrenching tool and one hundred rounds of
ammunition. The Rifles were billeted in
Hersham, and the other battalions in the
Brigade were all in the neighbourhood. The
others were put into private houses, but our
Colonel would not hear of it for some reason,
so we went into schools and institutes. The
people of Hersham were very disappointed;
all the villagers, shopkeepers, squire and
everybody else were prepared to take us, and
to give every man a bed, having laid in extra
provisions too. They kept on offering us
beds, and many fellows got dinners and teas
in the cottages, the occupiers of which
absolutely refused payment.

After eating our cold ration from our mess
tins on arrival, Tunnicliff, Rowmer, Stack
and I bought a loaf, some fish-paste, and pine-

apple, and made tracks for T.'s tent by the river Mole. The tent was still up, and he had butter, tea, marmalade and other stores there, so we had a good meal, after a glorious swim in the river, which did us a lot of good. The people at the farm loaded us up with apples; we filled our towels with them, 300 at least, enough for all the Company.

August 23rd, Sunday.

Friday night was cold, and sleeping, or trying to, on the bare floor, we felt the need of blankets. Yesterday's march from Hersham here to Bisley was very trying. It was hot and dusty, we were heavily loaded up, and the way was long. Two hundred and fifty men fell out from the other three battalions, but only four of the Rifles,[1] and none from our company. The people all the way along were full of sympathy and help for the stragglers, and I think these chaps quite enjoyed it. The reception we had all along the route was really wonderful. All of us had more apples than we could eat (and there were 4,000 men on the march), and plums,

---

[1] Three of them caught up later.

pears, cake and milk were pressed on us as we passed, or when we halted. People came running out of their houses with jugs of water for the troops, and altogether made an absurd fuss of us. We are under canvas with the rest of the T.F. Division (except four battalions who are supposed to be guarding the L.B. & S.C.R., and part of the South-Western Railway) at Bisley, on the National Rifle Association ground. There is very little spare time except on Sundays, and writing is difficult. Strict Regular discipline is enforced, and you may have to address your best friend as 'Corporal', and jump to an order. They have fairly caught us now. We are sleeping twelve in a tent, which with rifles, equipment, kit-bags, and food, is a squeeze. We have each a blanket. Réveillé is at six, and we may not leave the N.R.A. boundaries without a pass.

The Bishop of London took the Brigade Church Parade this morning, wearing a service cap over his robes.

August 24th.

Washed my shirt and socks, scrubbing them over some boards; they needed it so!

August 25th.

On pioneer duty today, which means that I picked up paper, cigarette-ends, spent matches and other rubbish all over the camping ground, and erected some canvas screens round the washing benches. The day was very hot, and I had a soft time really, while the company has been sweating at drill in the heat.

It is a great thing for us, coming to Bisley, as every member of the Rifles is *ipso facto* a member of one of the leading Rifle Clubs here, so we can use the Club house for meals, and an occasional concert.

Today the newsboys are racing down the lines with flaming contents bills, 'Fall of Namur'. It only arouses a mild interest. It really is remarkable how oblivious we are to what is going on overseas. There is very little in the papers about the British Army, even if we had time to read them, and, anyway, we are too self-centred and interested in our job to worry much about the War.

August 26th.

Tonight we held an al-fresco concert outside the Rifle Club Hut, a really good pro-

c

gramme, no smutty stuff; and two or three part-songs very well done.

August 27th.

I am beginning thoroughly to enjoy myself, getting used to the discipline, and delighting in the open air and good fellowship. Food is good and improving.

August 28th.

Another concert last night. Cumberland, looking very tall and straight and handsome, sang Kipling's 'Follow me 'ome'. If well done, it always moves a soldier audience. I generally sing on these occasions.

Before breakfast we had the usual Swedish drill, and afterwards section and company drill. In the afternoon the company went for a 5 or 6-mile route march, and practised passing messages along the column, noticing names and other objects along the road, memorizing landmarks, and practised keeping well locked up and to the left. Sometimes we skirmish to and fro over the Stickledown ranges among the furze bushes, very hot and prickly.

The battalion has volunteered for foreign

service, and will go as a battalion. Eighty per cent volunteered, and of the remaining 20 per cent some have applied for commissions. We have started recruiting again to fill up from 800 to 1,000, so as to go at full strength. We are all congratulating ourselves.

No pressure was put on any man to volunteer. Each man was called out of the ranks by the Company Commander, and quietly said Yes or No to him; that was all that happened.

August 29th.

Rather a trying day. Exceedingly hot. Busy at judging distances, fire control, and company drill, Swedish drill, and semaphore. We dug 'trenches', supposedly under fire, lying face downwards and scratching out a shelter with our little entrenching tools—a frightful sweat.

August 30th, Sunday.

The Bishop preached a sort of 'Holy War' appeal.

In the afternoon was fortunate in securing a pass, and met my people at Brookwood, and had tea with them in a cottage. After tea the party was broken up by an urgent recall of all details to camp, fellows flying round on cycles to collect us all. I think my poor mother thought we were off to France that minute, but it appeared that Lord Kitchener was in the neighbourhood. He did not come nearer than Divisional Head-quarters. Panic for nothing.

August 31st.

Attack practice over the heather this morning. Sir Ian Hamilton, Inspector-General, came down to look at us this afternoon.

September 1st.

Still very hot, though the early mornings are cold and misty. This morning a biplane soared over the camp, not very high up, a beautiful golden colour against a deep blue sky. We often see the Beta airship. Full moon and a glorious starlit night.

Here is the battalion on route march. A long khaki column headed by the Colonel on his horse, our rifles slung, greatcoats rolled on our backs with mess-tin in its canvas cover perched on them, sleeves rolled up, tunics

unbuttoned at the throat, caps on the backs
of our heads, sweat trickling down into our
eyes, and making runnels in the caked dust
on our faces, we swing along through the
dusty hedgerows, singing:

> 'Old King Cole was a merry old soul,
> And a merry old soul was he.
> He called for his pipe
> And he called for his bowl
> And he called for his captains three.
>
> 'Now each of the captains
>   Was a very fine captain;
> And a very fine cheek had he.
> "Can I go on leave for a year?" said the captain.
>   "I do all the work," said the subaltern.
> "Move to the right in fours," said the sergeant.
> "Bring me a quart of beer," said the corporal. . . .'

And so on.

September 3rd.

The nights are becoming as cold as the days
are hot, and a thick mist smothers us till half-
past eight, when the sun comes through and
scorches.

After breakfast we struck camp to air the
ground, pitching tents again before dinner.
An exhausting morning, flopping on furze
bushes. Officially this manœuvre is known

as Advancing by Short Rushes in Extended
Order. We are presumed to be attacking a
position, and are supposed to be up and down
again before our opponents can take a steady
aim. First one group goes, then another.
You scramble to your feet from a prone
position, and run forward for all you are
worth, till the leader signs with his hand, and
down you go on your stomach in the furze
and heather, the former pricking your hands
and legs most damnably. You lie there face
down gripping your rifle, and waiting for
the whistle that means the next advance, with
your equipment weighing you down, and
the sweat making your eyes smart. After a
morning of this you have earned your beer.

On returning to camp the first thing to do
is to change the wet shirt, have a drink and
scramble for some dinner in the tent; and when
the afternoon work is finished, a bucket bath,
tea, and content.

September 4th.

A longish march to our training ground,
past the Yeomanry camp; they are off to
Egypt on Sunday, with pith helmets. We
saw three troop-trains full of K.'s Army

recruits, in strange clothing, a mixture of civilian clothes, and slops from the Army rag-bag.

September 5th.

Vaccinated today; the Medical Officer did 100 men in an hour, which is pretty smart work. We filed bare-armed past him, were scratched with a nasty little implement, and the lymph was applied.

I went for a run in the evening with about a dozen men in the company over the heather behind the ranges, about three or four miles. Another glorious night.

September 6th.

Church Parade was a farce for our company; we did not hear one single word. The last hymn was a special one to the tune of 'The Church's One Foundation'; but the printed words did not go very far back. So the rear companies sang the usual words to the tune. The result was that as the A. and M. hymn has five verses, and the special one only four, the rear companies lustily sang a verse unaccompanied by the band—of the wrong hymn.

Tunnicliff had a hamper down today by rail, which must have cost quite £2—a great box from Teetgen's—two men had all they could do to carry it. We have accumulated mountains of food in our tent.

My father and mother and young brother came to see me today. The latter turned up in Boy Scout rig, and I gave him tea in the tent. He enjoyed this, and chummed up with Fender. I had tea with my people in the Rifle Club Hut.

September 7th.

This afternoon we were told we were to start for Crowborough tomorrow. The Aldershot Command is required for K.'s Army, so H.Q. Staff goes to Canterbury, and we move to the Canterbury area. At least, so says rumour, but anyhow it doesn't matter. Bisley is needed to teach the Kitchener recruits musketry. Great bustle in camp; frantic consumption of hampers.

September 8th.

Leaving piles of food behind for our successors in neat and orderly heaps, we started at 8 a.m. this morning, and marched about

14 miles to Horsley Towers, at East Horsley.
The whole division (save one brigade now in
Malta) is on the move. The left-half bat-
talion of the Rifles were at East Horsley,
some in the out-houses of the 'Duke of
Wellington', some in barns, woodsheds, and
yards attached to Horsley Towers. The
House itself is Divisional H.Q.

At first I, with some two dozen other men,
was put into a small dark stable behind the
inn, paved abominably with cobbles (fancy
lying on them!)—inhabited already by a
horse and some chickens, and with no windows.
Lieutenant Johns came round to inspect,
apparently disliked the look of it, and called
the captain, who shifted us to an open cart-
shelter in the Towers grounds. We moved
gratefully to this bivouac, a shelter over our
heads, open at the sides; and we piled heaps
of bracken on the ground for bedding. I
took off my boots and socks and jacket, put
my feet into the sleeves, piled bracken on
top, and my feet were warm. Then with
my two shirts on (I always carry a spare shirt
and pair of socks wrapped in my overcoat) I
wrapped myself in my greatcoat among the
bracken, and was soon asleep.

After billeting was complete, the cooks produced tea, and we made a meal off bread, and a ration issue of a mixture of stewed beef, beans, carrots and gravy, which we ate cold out of a round tin; tasted good.

Later we had a swim in a large pool, surrounded by tall beeches. Followed a drink and a rest; and Rowmer, Tunnicliff and I managed to buy at the village shop some unsweetened bottled gooseberries and biscuits, which we ate for supper; and so to bed, as already described.

September 9th.

Slept well; rose at 5.30; another swim. We had for breakfast bread and jam and tea (no milk) and a leg of bacon, which we cut up in the yard. We had to grub around for wood, light fires, and fry our own portions in our mess-tins.

I am writing this on Reigate Heath, while the local Boy Scouts are being told off to act as guides to our billets. We came through Dorking, round the foot of Box Hill. One cannot appreciate scenery much on these occasions, one sees principally Dust and Boots.

Everyone is very cheery, and we sing when the going is good. I am never troubled with my feet, but the 100 rounds of ammunition pull terribly at your shoulders.

At the halts we sing choruses, in harmony. Favourites are:

'Where my Caravan has rested.'

'Sweet and Low.'

'Annie Laurie.'

'I'm Ninety-Five' (the regimental quick-step).

'The Marseillaise.'

'Swanee River.'

And a fortissimo chant:

> 'Hoch der Kaiser,
> Donner und Blitzen,
> Salmon and Gluckstein,
> A-a-a-a-a-ch!!'

We are all very childish; Oranges and Lemons with crossed rifles; and all sorts of rot we get up to; nursery rhymes with the children, and so on.

The company is billeted in a small church hall. Rather a squash, and it means pigging it for meals. People are most kind. We always get fruit and food pressed upon us on the march, and often in the towns they won't

take payment for small things. I have had
my mess-tin scoured out with hot water at a
cottage here, and a hot bath and a shave at
the vicarage. We had a free swim at the
Public Baths. People are sending in great
baskets of apples and pears.

September 10th.

Quite a red-letter day for Reigate; there
were 5,000 men, foot and guns, quartered in
the town. We were on the move by 8 a.m.,
en route for East Grinstead. It rained heavily
last night for a change.

We are now halted about 2½ miles from
East Grinstead in a big meadow, and are about
to have our meal.

In a narrow road near Burstow Park we
were called to attention, and Eyes Right given,
and there was the King in khaki, standing at
the end of a little group of our field officers,
with half a dozen farm hands hanging over
a gate. He seemed to be scanning the ranks
very closely, and looked worn and tired. He
commented, so we hear, on our marching to
our C.O. who was standing by him, saying
it was better than the others. We only lost
one man today, and he was chivvied and

helped along, so we didn't really lose him; while from the other battalions men dropped by the road all the way.

We are billeted in the town. Twenty of us are in the billiard-room of the Railway Hotel. On arrival we had a swim in the open-air bath.

September 11th.

Raining hard; route march 'off'. Likely to be here some days. Rumour says there is no water laid on at Crowborough. We are not allowed about the town, and have to stay in billets this morning, which is rather dull. However, we have the billiard-table; and we were allowed out later for a while.

Paid today. The Rifles look a ragged, dirty lot. I shall be glad when our new uniforms and equipment arrive. After tea Rowmer and Tunnicliff dragged me to the Cinema. We always hang together, and there was certainly nothing else to do.

The almost entirely military audience amused itself by spotting the frequent mistakes in films of a military character, and there was a running fire of humorous comment on all the pictures.

September 12th, Saturday.

Very cold last night. Hope blankets will soon arrive. Brigade route march, about 10 miles into the beautiful Ashdown Forest country. Felt we needed a hot bath, so Rowmer, Tunnicliff, and I called at the work-house, and asked for one. We were given an excellent bath in the Infants' Department, with toys in the bath to play with. A nurse had taken some trouble in preparing the baths for us, so afterwards we went and bought some flowers, which we brought back and presented to her. To our surprise she seemed only half pleased. Perhaps she didn't like accepting anything from 'common soldiers'. You never know with women. Mending and washing socks this evening.

September 13th, Sunday.

Blankets arrived, so we slept warm last night. Church Parade in the Parish Church. The Bishop of London preached, and read a letter 'from the trenches', all about German outrages. The Law forbids billiards on Sunday, although the billiard-room is our temporary home! We are told the behaviour of the troops here has been exceedingly good, and the Grinstead people are full of compliments.

Rather interesting yesterday to see the brigade on the march. We were at the head of the column of route, and once, on the top of a ridge, we could look back over our shoulders and see winding away a mile-long brown column. A grand view over valley and forest. Tunnicliff looks after our inner man. He likes shopping for its own sake, and says he likes to see everything in its proper place, and the proper place for food is inside, not lying about in shops.

September 14th.

This stay at East Grinstead is a holiday— a 10-mile march in the morning, and the rest of the day to ourselves; you can swim, stroll, play billiards, write letters, or eat. The people of the inn often make us soup or puddings.

September 15th.

Outpost work—glorious country—was acting Corporal today.

September 16*th.*

We have marched away to a most beautiful site, Camp Hill, in Ashdown Forest, 650 feet up, with grand views of heather and fir and pine and the distant line of the South Downs. But no preparations have been made for us and nobody loves us. When we halted, we put on our greatcoats, piled arms, and lay down on the hill-side. Being cold and windy weather, we built a fire at the end of the lines, and sat round it in heaps. We ate some bread and cheese, and a little bully beef (saved from a 6 a.m. breakfast), and later on the cook served us stew, which was burnt, with no vegetables or bread. This was at three o'clock, and we have had nothing else today except a mug of tea. As it grew dark, the tents and a few blankets arrived, and we started to pitch. There was a shortage of pegs, and we only had four in our tent-party, so I crept up in the dusk to tents that had a better allowance and stole some. I got three or four this way, and later four more were issued, and then I scouted about the camp for bits of wood, and cut six more with a knife. We used our bayonets for brailing pegs. The kit-bags arrived, so I had a sweater, but we had no blankets in our tent.

September 17th.

Very early in the morning it rained and blew, and it is still doing so (11.30 a.m.). No bread for breakfast, only a little fat ham, and tea, but later on we each had half a dozen fancy lunch biscuits. Hope dinner will be more successful, though cooking in this terrible weather must be difficult. We are very exposed; the soil is black sand like Camberley;[1] the weather is wet and stormy like Lulworth;[1] it is cold; no parcels and no canteen, and other active-service privations. But we don't care; we shall often be worse off than this.

I have just come in from helping to dig gullies and trenches round the tent to carry off the water. I have never had to do that before in all my camping experience, but we are on a slope. This black sand makes us very dirty, but though there is too much water, we cannot wash as there are no buckets. Haven't washed for 48 hours. But then on active service I suppose one doesn't reckon to wash more than once a week, if one is lucky.

[1] Peace-time summer camps.

D

Dinner arrived at 2.15, boiled mutton, but no bread or potatoes. A little cheese, and later on a few biscuits. However, it kept us going. Then the clouds blew away; and left blue sky and a great wind. All was clear again, and we saw the Martello Towers on Pevensey Bay, the Downs, and the sea.

Tea was just tea in a mug, but providentially a huge cake arrived for Rowmer, so we were all right. Had a shave and some sort of a wash before tea, but am now dirty again. We look like a lot of sweeps.

All the evening from long after dark I have been out with a party from the tent cutting sods with heather with our entrenching tools, to form a floor for the tent and get rid of the black sand. A parcel of food has come at last. We have now a bucket and more pegs.

September 18th.

Food still rather short, but we bought some cake from a hawker. Bitterly cold here on the hill-top, especially mornings and nights, but the air is invigorating, and I feel very well. Views glorious. One can see the run of the Downs from Eastbourne to Chanctonbury, and Shoreham Gap; Pevensey

Bay, Firle and Ditchling Beacons, Lewes
Castle, the Devil's Dyke, and all the Weald
between. Northward is East Grinstead and
beyond the chalk escarpments of the North
Downs, and at night the glow of London. A
cardigan jacket has arrived just when badly
wanted.

September 19th.

Mighty cold this morning. Did some
attacks over the open scrub—rather an interesting morning. An old sergeant cook
from Aldershot with 20 years' service at the
job has turned up, and signalized his presence
by giving us hot bacon for breakfast, and
roast beef and potatoes for dinner. We shall
be all right now. Our tent is very snug, with
the heather sods and piles of bracken.

September 20th, Sunday.

The Bishop took a Communion Service in
the great Y.M.C.A. marquee. Canvas flap-
ping in the keen morning air, and the sun
breaking through; now and again bugle calls
and distant words of command. After dinner
got passes, and went for a walk with Eveson
and Tunnicliff, one of the finest walks I have

ever been, through Five Hundred Acre Wood (oak and pine and forest pool) to Hartfield, Withyham (where we had tea) and Buckhurst Park.

September 21st.

Marched out on the Maresfield Road and turned off to Nutley. Did an attack over some very beautiful (and very prickly) country; and again in the evening, collecting more prickles. Bathing from a bucket of cold water in the evening on the bare hillside is a chilly business in this cold wind.

September 22nd.

This morning digging real trenches with picks and shovels, not the scrapes made with entrenching tools. Disguised them with sods and gorse bushes. Selected to attend promotion class; hope to get my stripe soon. Am now drawing 3d. a day efficiency pay. Saw a kestrel hovering over the trenches and found a brown lizard and a grass snake.

September 23rd.

Killed a large viper this morning. Short night march this evening. The regiment has now put up a recreation marquee with tables and deck chairs, also a wet and dry canteen.

September 24th.

This morning we drew rations of beef, potatoes, and bread, which we are to cook in our mess-tins. I am writing this in the warm sunshine on the top of a hill. Am in charge of a squad which is keeping communication between a standing patrol and the main picket a thousand yards away. Behind me the patrol is lying in wait for the enemy scouts who are creeping up. Was teaching semaphore to a squad this morning while we were waiting for the 'enemy' to get out to their position. We cooked our own dinners in the field, each man making his own little fire. I made a stew of my ration of lumps of beef and two potatoes, enriched with an Oxo cube, a Brand's Essence tablet, and half a packet of desiccated soup. Dug a tiny trench, and made a wee fire of twigs, simmering the concoction in water from my water-bottle. Got it all going with one match, and by taking a little trouble it turned out good and tender.

September 25th.

Brigade march this morning—Chuck Hatch, Hartfield, and Coleman's Hatch—9 miles. Rowmer left us today to our great regret, having applied for a commission. He was in the same tent as I was during our first year with the regiment seven years ago, when we discovered we had been at the same school; and we have been close pals ever since.

September 27th.

My mother and father came to see me to-day. I met them at Jarvis Brook Station, and took them to Redbridge Farm, where we had an excellent lunch. It was delightful to eat a civilized meal again. Then we went for a stroll in the woods, sat down, and talked for a while. They want me to apply for a commission, but I do not want to leave the regiment. I am sorry for these two dear people. They are so good and brave, but I know there is black anxiety behind their quiet demeanour. A beautiful sunny day; the woods very still and quiet.

September 28th.

Out all day from 9 to 5. Only just over an hour to build and light our fires, cook our dinners, and eat them, and clear up. I had a piece of steak, so decided to fry it, that being the quickest way to deal with it. Having some fat it was a success, only had to eat it too fast. Boiled the potatoes in the other half of the mess-tin.

The Bishop was out with us today, thoroughly enjoying himself. The wind got up, and they had a real dust-storm in camp, so we were well out of it.

September 29th.

Another heavy day. Eight-mile march in the morning as an advance-guard. I was in charge of flankers, and had to run about a lot. After dinner, semaphore practice, then promotion class. A rush back for tea, and immediately I paraded with some others as an 'enemy' against the rest of the company for night operations. That meant 7 miles more, much of it running and crawling. After the show was over, we helped to put out a heath fire, and turned in at 11 p.m. after eleven hours' duty.

September 30th.

Today we were defending a position on a ridge. Made a military sketch-map of the terrain. I was inoculated against typhoid this afternoon—a sharp prick with a hypodermic syringe. My arm was very stiff and sore afterwards.

October 1st.

Felt stiff and cold and shivery, the effect of the inoculation. This evening we have been changing the bracken and thoroughly disinfecting everything with Izal, a bottle of which we procured recently.

Dust is the only drawback to this camp. The tents are quite black, and the wits write names in the dust on the tents, e.g. 'Dustbin Lodge', 'New Scotland Yard' (where the Corporal of Regimental Police lives), 'No Hawkers, no Circulars', and such-like.

October 2nd.

The Bishop left us today; we gave him a rousing send-off, for he has made himself very popular.

October 3rd.

Luxurious hot bath at a house called Pound-
gate, owned by a Mr. Longridge. They
invited me to dinner afterwards. The effect
of the bath was truly extraordinary; much of
the 'sunburn' washed off!

October 4th.

I have been looking through our larder in
the tent. About 20 pounds of marmalade,
3 pounds of jam, a large supply of butter,
5 very large cakes, 4 tins of Nestle's milk,
sausages, sausage rolls, tarts, 6 large cans of
pineapple, a flagon of Burgundy, a quantity
of apples, fish-paste, and a lot of odds and
ends. We hardly know what to do with the
hampers that reach us from all our friends.

October 5th.

These notes are dull. Lots of amusing
things happen, but they are trifles which are
nothing written down. For instance, when
after this morning's attack we were having
the usual pow-wow, Mr. Johns made some
little joke, the pack-horse threw up his head
and neighed a long loud laugh, full of de-

rision and contempt. Nothing to tell, but extremely funny at the time.

October 6th.

Clarendon Hotel, Tunbridge Wells. The Company has just marched here, and is having a good dinner in the billiard-room and other rooms. Much of the route was through woods of oak and pine and beech. The autumn colours are ripening and deepening every day. We kept passing traction engines, with wagons loaded with timber, for building hutments at Crowborough, I suppose. We have had a hot bath and a swim. Tunnicliff and I have had a close crop at a barber's. Then we had a coffee on the Pantiles, tasted the waters, rejoined, and marched home again. About 21 miles today.

October 7th.

Magnificent sunrise; the sun shot up blazing red just opposite our tent door. I sleep by the door, as I like as much air as possible, and we leave the flap open. (I write during a wayside halt.) It is a glorious morning. A gentle south-easterly breeze is coming from the sea, which is gleaming seven leagues away.

Mile after mile of woods stretch away to the Downs, and the clear sunshine reveals all the green hollows of the hills. The stretches of moorland are dark gorse and brown bracken, and in the woods the oak and beech are burning red and gold.

October 8th.

Last night we practised spotting men walking about in front of us in the dark; and putting on our kits and assembling without any sound. Then we made a silent night assault on a position. We formed company column from column of fours; then extended to single rank, fixing bayonets as we went; and in four lines ran quietly up the hill.

October 9th.

A foxhound that attached itself to us on the march to the Wells is still with us. He lives on scraps from the officers' mess, and did rather too well the first day, getting his tail down a bit. However, he has now been sick in the adjutant's tent, and feels much better. He parades with us in the morning. This afternoon we had a practice alarm. We fell in for roll-call, in marching order, the transport limbered up, the cooks packed up, and the whole battalion was ready to move off.

October 10th.

Today we practised digging ourselves in with entrenching tools—the ones we carry on us. It has been found in France and Belgium that the narrow scrapes giving head cover were not enough, as shrapnel gets the men in the legs, so we have to scoop out an egg-shaped hole and lie crouched up.

October 12th.

Inoculated again against typhoid. About three-quarters of an hour afterwards, while having tea in the tent, I suddenly felt as if a bucket of cold water had been poured over me, teeth chattering so that I could hardly speak.

The pay from mobilization of a rifleman is 1s. 8d. a day (1s. pay, 2d. for kit allowance, and 6d. proficiency pay).

This morning the company struck tents, and took them away until we found a heathery place where we beat them with pine branches, and shook them till they were quite free from dust. Then we scraped all the surface of the ground, watered it, and re-pitched.

October 13th.

Things rather miserable, as it is raining and we are suffering from the inoculation. Wish we had floor-boards, everything gets so dirty.

I heard today that already 50 per cent of the office staff are with the Colours. They called up 100 new men from the waiting list, but only about a dozen responded.

October 15th.

Started battalion training. Mostly drill today, with a night march through the woods. In bayonet fighting we have to forget the School of Arms finesse; just vigorous thrusts, two parries, and a firm grip.

October 16th.

Recommended for promotion to lance-corporal. In the evening Tunnicliff and I walked to Crowborough to try and get a hot bath at the Crest Hotel (6d. each for soldiers), but there were fourteen waiting, so we went away and had some tea. We returned through the Warren Woods, dark as pitch.

October 17th.

Appointed lance-corporal (unpaid). To-night Tunnicliff and I got our bath at the Crest. We arrived at 4, and our turn came at 5.40.

Hutments are going up fast, men working night and day against the coming of winter.

The other day it was very hot and we were sitting all dusty by the roadside, when a large motor-lorry passed laden with casks of beer. The company sprang to its feet as one man and presented arms, to the joy of the rosy old brewers' men.

October 18th, Sunday.

The text of the sermon at Church Parade was, 'How goodly are thy tents, O Israel!' Ours is generally smothered with dust, except when it rains, and then there is mud over everything. Yet it is our home, and we are quite fond of it. Another luncheon party in the woods. Peggy Tunnicliff sewed on my stripes properly for me, and gave me a lesson in renewing buttonholes.

This evening I went for a solitary walk in the still dark woods, black and gold in the sunset, dim and intensely quiet in the twilight.

It is an order that all men shall provide themselves with an abdominal belt of knitted wool.

October 19th.

I was orderly corporal today, which means a busy time. You parade the sick, and all fatigue parties and orderlies, and parade for letters, being generally responsible for the food, comfort, and well-being of the company.

October 20th.

Floor-boards arrived at last.

October 21st.

Rained hard at night, but broke fair in the morning; an autumn day at its best. We swung along breathing deep the fresh clean air for about 4 miles, when we suddenly had the order to deploy. The idea of course was that we had suddenly come under heavy artillery fire. We pressed on in diamond formation of sections, eventually extended, and pushed home an attack. It was very rough country, plenty of hard running, but I felt so fit that I could have run for an hour and marched till dark. On the way home the skipper suddenly shouted, 'Aeroplane!' and we all dashed like rabbits for the side of the road, and lay flat down in the ditches under the hedge.

More bayonet instruction this afternoon. Our chaps are beginning to hold their weapons as if they meant business. Wetted my stripe today at dinner in the tent with drinks all round, and took the opportunity to intimate that I was to be addressed as 'Corporal' in future, and not by my name or nickname. This sort of thing is awkward with old friends, but it is just like it was at school; if you are in authority and people get too familiar, they will argue when told to do something they don't like, and arguing is barred with a war on.

The first-aid outfit bought in Crowborough the other day came in useful this afternoon. A man cut his head open on someone's rifle, and I was able to patch him up.

October 22nd.

Strong sou'wester blowing, with lashings of rain. Two pick-up games, Rugger and Soccer; I played in the former, and chanced my knee. We played in our trousers, put–

tees, and shirts, just as we were, in the pouring rain, all very wet and muddy and happy.

October 23rd.

Still a sou'wester with rain. The company paraded with picks and shovels for trench digging, working at it till 5 o'clock. We made little pillars every 3 yards in a parapet and parados, with poles and cross-slats to take sods of turf. It is then supposed to be shrapnel-proof. It was quite a work of art, with a drain, a gangway, a firestep, and neatly measured off, and it was a pity to have to fill it in.

This evening about 20 of us had tea together, it being Founder's Day. We talked about school-days and school-ways and changes; old times and new; also of Old Blues in Navy and Army. We drank the old toast, 'To the Religious Royal and Ancient Foundation of Christ's Hospital. May those prosper who love it and may God increase their number.'

October 25th, Sunday.

On leave today for the first time. Saw my father and mother and Philip, and Kath-

E

leen came up from Dover. Since East Grinstead days I have been corresponding again
with Norah in Canada; believe she is home
again now.

October 26th.

More musketry instruction; I generally
have a little squad to talk to. We have been
lining a shallow trench, practising fire control. View glorious; the whole stretch of
weald and down, and northwards across the
forest 9 miles away is East Grinstead standing out sharply, and beyond, the chalk North
Downs.

October 28th, Wednesday.

At 6.30 this morning the orderly sergeant
came down the lines with the news that we
were leaving England for an 'unknown destination'—France, I suppose—on Saturday.

Orderly sergeant's bugle call keeps going.
The neighbouring battalion is very curious;
we are elated, and I think inwardly rather
excited.

Last night there was a brigade 'practice'
alarm, all four battalions with transport and
all details; we marched away some distance
and then returned to bed.

October 29th.

Rained hard last night; wakened us several times. Réveillé at 5.30; we threw back our blankets, lighted a candle, and struggled into our clothes. Breakfast was at 6, with parade at 7; no time for wash or shave.

Dawn was stormy, saffron yellow merging into pale blue, with tumbled masses of purple cloud. We marched straight out to the ranges. It was now bright and clear, a blue sky with one long ridge of rosy cloud along the south. Over the reddening forest the mists were rolling away like battle-smoke.

We fired 5 rounds slow, then 15 rounds in one minute at 200 yards. This last is the Regular soldier's test, and it takes some doing. I managed to fire all mine in the time and get them all on the target. The senior corporal and I tied for top score of the section; the same score in both practices and shot for shot together in the rapid. After firing, had my forgone 'bucket-bath' and shave. Now raining in torrents. Fifty foreign service recruits are down from the 2nd Battalion.

October 30*th, Friday.*

Rained in sheets again in the night; my blankets got wet. Leave home today from Réveillé to Lights Out. Went to the office, drew some money, and greeted those few left whom I know. Thence to see Harry; next to H.Q. to have a look at the 2nd Battalion. Rowmer was acting 'colour-bloke', and it being Friday, was busy with the pay-sheets in the sergeants' mess. We had a long talk there. The whole 2nd Battalion has volunteered for foreign service.

Then I called on Oscar Wakefield and went home to a bath and a meal at noon. My mother and father are absolute bricks. They know I am going overseas, and they take it splendidly. I am grateful; it makes it so much easier for me.

October 31*st.*

New rifles, equipment, clothing, and boots issued today. The rifle is the old pattern (long) adapted for Mark VII ammunition, and the trajectory is flat up to 600 yards. A fine weapon, but the Regular short rifle is handier. I hear the officers are to carry packs and rifles like ourselves. What a revolution! Writing this in the dark, on the edge of a pine wood, in charge of a picket.

November 1st.

Went to early service in the church tent, and said good-bye to Canon Pearce.[1] After breakfast Sergeant Eveson and I went for a long tramp to Maresfield, Fletching, and Nutley to see the last of Old England. We lunched at Fletching: at the 'Griffin' where Bernard and I went last June—bread and cheese and some wonderful home-made cider, very powerful. Typical Sussex views on this walk, humpy downs on the sky-line, rolling tree-clad weald in front, and just ahead a strip of white road and a mass of trees, throwing back the distant prospect. A marvellous clear sunny day.

Studying some French maps this evening.

November 3rd.

Inspected by Major-General Fry, who said he had never seen a physically finer battalion. He recalled the doings of the Rifle Brigade in the Peninsular War, as an example for us. Good old London Scottish have been in a scrap at Messines. They

[1] Later Bishop of Worcester.

weren't very long; I wonder how soon we shall be in action. We have been ordered to move off today; had the orders cancelled; warned for an alarm; had our passes stopped; had our foreign orders cancelled; had our passes and foreign orders renewed; and now have orders to move tomorrow. Great minds are at work.

November 4th.

Writing this in the troop-train. We had a great send-off from camp by the other battalions who lined the road for us, and were played along by one of their bands on our 5-mile march to the station. They played 'Swanee River', 'Tipperary', 'The Girl I left behind me', and 'Who'll come to France with me?' and 'Auld Lang Syne', as the train steamed out, a memorable experience. I shall never forget the mingled emotions of those moments, the poignancy of the throbbing music, and the cheers with which we expressed our exhilaration on being really embarked on a great adventure.

November 4th (evening).

We ran right alongside the sheds at Southampton and embarked at once. Breathing

in the cool salt air after the stuffy train we
became aware of several other troopships
getting under way, dim shapes in the darkness. A searchlight stabbed through the
night, wheeled, and was gone. A great shout
floated over the water, hundreds of voices
in unison—'ARE—WE—DOWNHEARTED?' an-
swered by our thunderous 'NO!'

Our ship was a B.I. liner. There was a
great crush below; we were accommodated
for the night in horse-boxes with corrugated
floors: excessively uncomfortable. Got some
hot water from the lascars.

November 5th, Thursday.

Have just passed the Havre light-ship. A
calm crossing, and day broke very fine. At
7 a.m. tea and hard thick biscuits, like dog
biscuits, were issued. Last night we were
passed by a hospital ship, a fast trim liner with
two funnels, a beautiful sight, lit from end
to end, with a big red cross painted amidships
and illuminated. She steamed right into a
searchlight from one of the forts. We sailed
with ports closed and no lights.

Le Havre is a clean-looking white town at
the foot of a long line of cliffs. After dis-

embarking, we had a very trying march for about 5 miles up-hill, carrying with us rations of canned beef and biscuits. The weight on our backs, a more or less sleepless night, hunger, thirst, and the reaction of yesterday made us feel very weary, and we were utterly thankful when we reached the rest camp at last.

The town seemed curiously quiet considering its importance and size, but the people were very pleased to see us, especially the children, who tried to shake hands with us all, and ran along shouting, 'Souvenir', 'Biscuit', and 'Good night' (a universal greeting this). One old woman as I passed drew her hand across her throat and screamed, 'Coupez la gorge des boches!' and another, with the same gesture cried, 'À bas Guillaume, à bas Guillaume!'

The French bayonet is a murderous-looking affair, about twice the length of ours, and very thin and snaky. I was unlucky in being in charge of a party drawing stores, which meant much wandering about the town and heavy carrying work, so was dog-tired when at last we turned into marquees —66 men in ours, no room to turn over.

Many of our fellows had no tents at all, and had to spend a frosty night on the grass.

November 6th.

Had an all-over wash in a sun like August. This afternoon we bivouacked for a few hours in the goods yard of the station—Gare des Marchandises. A striking scene in the dusk, piled rifles, men sitting about on their packs, the cooks feeding a great blaze with broken ration-boxes, and making tea. We entrained about 8.30 p.m. in covered trucks, marked '40 hommes, 8 chevaux'. There are 33 or 34 men in our truck, which with packs and rifles is about all it can hold.

November 7th.

Have been slam-banging about all night, and still far to go; rather chilly. We have blacked over our white-metal hat-badges. By the way, an order has been issued forbidding us to part with them to civilians. Apparently the Regulars have been doing this, but it seems most unsoldierly. There are numbers of French Boy Scouts to be seen in the familiar uniform.

I often used to wonder, before the war, if

the regiment ever saw active service, how we would feel and behave. Probably it is due to the confidence born of our recent training, but it appears to affect neither our sleep, appetite, nor spirits in the least. Everybody smokes, reads, plays cards, or chats as unconcernedly as possible. Personally, I feel less excited and interested than when travelling down to play in some important Rugger match. I think we all treat it as a bit of a game, and I am quite sure we shall give a good account of ourselves. We have seen a number of gaily-dressed French and North African cavalrymen.

7 p.m. Train halted at last, after a day and a night, at St. Omer. After hanging about for a while, we marched to some cavalry barracks, very old disreputable whitewashed narrow buildings—stables below, and men above—they look as if the great Napoleon's men had used them, and they had never been cleaned up since. However, our room was strewn with some clean straw, and we all fell asleep almost at once.

Sanitation in these barracks is an absolute disgrace. There appears to be about one privy to a block, never cleaned, and, of course, quite innocent of any flushing apparatus. I think the French must be a dirty lot in these matters. One cannot dimly imagine English barracks in such a state, at all events in these days.

November 8th.

St. Omer is a quaint old place with narrow streets and large cobbles. There is a fine Gothic cathedral, standing hard by the ruins of an earlier one, the tower of which still stands. We marched out about 4 miles to a large empty convent at the village of Wisques; a very comfortable roomy billet, though with neither light nor heat laid on.

I am now in a very large lofty bare room. Here and there is a treasured flickering candle. Round the wall you can distinguish men lying on the bare boards—we are 70 in here —and little groups are chatting or playing cards round a candle, which throws uneven light on the faces, and great shadows on the whitewashed walls. Packs and equipments are lined along the walls, and rifles are stacked in the corners. Benson has just offered to bet me that the war will be over by Christmas. I took him on.

The only drawback to this billet is the lack of water—no washing arrangements, in fact, no water is laid on to the place at all, as far as we can discover. This morning I poured a little water from my water-bottle into the lid of my mess-tin, first cleaned my teeth in it, then shaved with it, and then, with the aid of a rubber sponge, washed in it.

Just now some men with flute and whistles are leading wild dances and choruses. We are quite cut off from news—we have no idea what is going on. We can see the low flickers of guns like far away lightning on the eastern horizon, and after a long time a series of dull rumbles, a faint shivering of the night air. Every evening a group of men is to be seen standing on a knoll before the convent, watching and listening; and they speak in low voices, their faces turned to the east—Ypres.

November 10th.

Digging reserve trenches some miles away —very wet. It is a weary, back-breaking job this navvying in the soaking yellow clay. We are reserve troops to the Regulars up in front, but I don't imagine we shall ever man these miserable ditches.

A well has been discovered near the billet —water fit for washing only. Tonight some of us stripped naked, and dashed out into the rain and wind; and then with the help of the rubber sponge had a bath in a biscuit tin.

Tobacco rations issued tonight. We can usually buy butter and bread and a little wine in the village. In odd moments we cut each other's hair. To use the clippers evenly requires quite a knack. We look very unprepossessing with our prison crops.

November 13th.

Don't think I have ever been more uncomfortable than I have been today, but I suppose I shall plumb yet further depths of misery! For we have come back to a fine hot meal and a warm room, or comparatively warm, at any rate, dry; but a few days later our quarters may be very much worse. However, we had some fun out of it, and all's well that ends well.

This was the programme: breakfast at 6, parade at 6.45, and more trench-digging. Raining and blowing and hailing all the time, we were soaked through, and plastered with mud; but now we have a hot stew and rum and tea. AH!

November 14th.

More trench-digging. Seems to me that everything we learnt at Crowborough and Bisley has been washed out. Methods of attack and trench-digging are quite different from those we have learnt, and the semaphore signalling we so laboriously acquired is apparently useless.

November 15th.

Wet again. Musketry practice. Everyone singing and cheerful; plenty of food.

November 16th.

Réveillé at 4.30 a.m., paraded very sleepily —we have had a heavy week. We left our convent for good, marching about 16 miles over unspeakable roads, either slush or terrible cobbles—*pavé*, as they call it—your feet slip under you. Arrived very weary; had a rum ration issued. Rum is wonderful stuff for warming and reviving. It goes down like a liquid flame and sends a glow through all one's veins.

The company struck a good billet. We were on the stage of a concert hall in Hazebrouck. Got an excellent meal at a little restaurant, best for weeks: steak, potatoes, omelette, bread, butter, jam, cheese, beer, syrups and coffee. Word was passed down the column on the march that Lord Roberts is dead—died at St. Omer.

November 17th.

Another march; more awful slithery roads, guns pounding away in front, and ever getting nearer. The blue sky strung with tufts of fleecy shrapnel—anti-aircraft. Am now in Bailleul—nice place—met the 3 Stanton brothers, who are here with the Artists' Rifles. Billeted in a large school.

November 18th.

They gave us a rest today. Saw some stragglers from the lines come limping in, incredibly dirty and played out. They had a fortnight's growth of beard, were plastered with mud from head to foot, greatcoats ragged and torn, some without arms, all barely able to drag one foot after another. They were hobbling back in small groups or

singly—quite a small number in all. Wonder
who and what they are, remnants of a defeated battalion, or stragglers that have lost
their units, and are making their own way
back? We gazed at them in wonder and
pity; hope we never come to look like that.

November 19th.

Snowing hard. Marched to a village called
Ploegsteert (anglicé Plugstreet). Billeted in
barns, lofts and cottages. I was congratulating myself on securing one of the latter,
when I was hauled out to take charge of nine
poor wretches in a loft, clean but dark and
perishing cold. However, we are better off
than the barn-dwellers. Am now having
coffee and chipped potatoes in an estaminet,
as they call the little pubs that abound in
these parts. 'Pommes de terre frites' is
anglicized into 'Bombardier Fritz' by the
Tommies.

November 20th.

Glorious morning, clear, bright and frosty,
snow everywhere. Near our billets were
two big howitzers cunningly concealed from
enemy aeroplane observation. It is fascina-

ting to watch aeroplanes being pursued by shrapnel. A tiny dot is probably all you see of the 'plane, and 'flick' goes a speck of white light, and a little white ball of fleecy smoke appears against the blue and hangs there. Another and another, till all round the 'plane hang these little white clouds.

Our platoon (we are adopting the Regular 4-company organization) started for the firing line at 3.30 p.m. We had a short march through a hamlet which had been shelled a few days ago, and which was an extraordinary sight, utterly desolate, and properly knocked about. Grand clear sunset over the snow. I can quite understand why Flanders has produced some great painters. We reached the reserve trenches (ripping cosy dug-outs, with head cover and plenty of straw) and turned into barns for an hour. Then, it being dark, we started along the road for the advanced trenches. Here we were under fire for the first time; German snipers a few hundred yards away put some bullets over our heads, chance pot-shots probably. Personally, I didn't feel a bit nervous; merely interested. I was pleased at that, because I didn't know how it would affect me.

F

While we were in billets this morning my party, mostly young soldiers, were inclined to be fidgety, and I found it necessary to be as merry and bright as possible. They probably hated me for this. They are all right now. Anticipation was worse than realization.

November 21st.

Writing this in the firing-line, with bullets going 'smack' against the parados behind, just over my head. Germans about 300 yards away from here.

My first night in the trenches was remarkably quiet, and things are distinctly dull this morning. We are with the Hampshires, learning the ropes, so to speak. We work in pairs at night, in shifts. One keeps watch, while his mate lies down in a little cave scooped out in front of the trench; two hours on and two hours off. Bayonets are kept fixed, of course, and magazines full, and now and then we take pot-shots over the top, for luck. Very little shelling. Half the night I was in charge of a little working party of ours and some Hants men engaged in digging a communication trench to the rear. The clay is

very stiff and frozen, and I was glad when
daylight came. Bullets whistled over constantly, but I don't think we could be seen
at that distance. However, once they put
3 shells down by us, and here was a little
problem for a new N.C.O. Had we been
heard or seen? And what to do? My in-
stinct was to carry on, though I should have
liked to knock off. The Regular Tommies
assured me that the usual practice was to
knock off for a spell to make sure there were
no more coming. I decided to lead them in,
and report to the Sergeant. He cursed me
for coming in, and told me to go back in ten
minutes, which we did till daylight. No
more shells. During the day one man in
eight keeps watch, while the others eat and
sleep. I am with Foot. We have rigged up
a little shelter with a waterproof sheet, and
have broken up a box for fuel. We light
little fires in our burrows or scoops, with
wood or charcoal, and make our own tea in
our mess-tins, or heat up the tinned stew
(known as Maconochie, from the firm that
makes it). Weather beautifully fine, but
awfully cold, especially at night. Snow everywhere.

We fill our water-bottles at a ruined farm at night, when the snipers cannot see us, and we have to make that do for the whole day.

The Regular Tommies are really great. They are up to all sorts of tricks, and are most cheery and amusing. They call the Germans 'Allymans' (French, *Allemands*) and shout to them, and make a lot of fun out of the business. But they do want to go home, and they all think the war will be over by Christmas, owing to the huge German losses. Every single man I have spoken to here says the same. I am afraid I don't think so; not so soon as that!

Just at the moment our guns somewhere back are putting some shrapnel over. They make a queer noise whirring over our heads.

I innocently asked a Regular, 'When do we attack?' His answer was full of amazement, mingled with scorn, and horror at the bare idea of such a thing. It appears that in this war both sides spend much of their time sitting in wet ditches waiting for the other fellow to begin.

November 22nd.

Last night we floundered out through an ice-bound slippery communication trench to the reserve line in the wood. Water in our water-bottles was frozen by the morning, but by lying close we kept fairly warm; had some straw. Quite a picnic; not so cramped here. A great crucifix stands amid the ruins of the hamlet (Le Gheer), the only thing undamaged. Incongruous with the bullets whistling round.

November 23rd.

Out digging half the night—very tired; rum ration most welcome. As you gulp it down it makes the blood run tingling all through your veins; a most delicious warming sensation when weary and wet. Some frost-bitten feet casualties. The enemy fired a light rocket at us, probably hearing the clink of our picks and spades, but we dropped down and crouched still, no harm being done; only a few wide pot-shots in our direction. Found some potatoes in a field. Two of the Regulars, one of ours, and a stretcher-bearer chased a cock-pheasant and bagged it for the pot, with a stick.

November 24th.

Back to H.Q.; barns; filthy billet. Billets in these parts smell. Imagine a rectangular midden full of steaming straw and muck, a brick pathway slippery with mud round it; at one end a farm-house with a savage dog everlastingly chained up in a narrow kennel, the remaining three sides of the midden flanked with barns and store-houses, with or without lofts, with heaps of muddy straw on the floors. This is where we live and sleep and eat, and we wash under the pump. But you do not drink the water because the midden no doubt drains into the supply. Tea is the soldiers' drink in the war, with beer occasionally, when you can get it.

November 26th.

More 'landscape gardening' in the wood. There is a path in the wood about half a mile behind the front line which we are making into a defensive line by digging a shallow trench and dumping bundles of brushwood into it in the vain hope that they will not sink into the mud. I am sure they will. The idea is to give some firm foothold on the floor.

We are also making corduroy paths up which
rations and supplies can go.

Front line again tonight.

November 27th.

Front line. It is thawing, with some rain;
and the parapets are beginning to slide into
the trench. Everything and everybody
plastered with mud: mud on your hands and
face, and down your neck and in your food,
and bits of mud in your tea. Terribly hard
to keep awake at night, especially between
12 and 3.30.

It is warmer now, and sunny; an occasional
bullet against the parapet or into the wood,
and now and then a 15-lb. shell, but on the
whole very quiet indeed.

The constant watching, standing, digging,
and repairs during the long 14½-hour night
is trying.

November 28th.

More rain, and the parapets slithering fast
into the trench. Repairs all the morning
instead of sleep. Either the tinned food, the
water, or the cold has made my stomach go
wrong, but a restriction of diet to bread and

tea is putting it right. Many others are the same. The cold seems to creep into your vitals. Our casualties to date are, I believe, two killed and three or four wounded.

My partner and I scraped a little hole in the side of the trench where we light our fire, for boiling tea and heating the meat and vegetable ration (Maconochie). The fuel is shavings cut with a pocket-knife from bits of old boxes, and a German bayonet stuck in the clay serves as a peg on which to hang our mess-tins.

November 30th.

Left trenches last night. After floundering and forcing our way along a narrow communication trench and slipping and sliding about over the open, we reached the barn at midnight, a terrible journey, worst experience I have ever had. The mud and our fatigue combined made it a nightmare. Several were absolutely knocked out, and all were not far off it. Loudoun collapsed completely, and carrying him and his kit made it worse. I finished fresher than most, and am perfectly fit today.

December 1st.

The Platoon Sergeant (Elsom), Lance-Corporal Benson (an old schoolfellow) and myself are transferred to No. 12 Platoon, so have to go up tomorrow night for an extra turn.

Today we had a HOT BATH in a small brewery in Ploegsteert—a great event. I hear the King is in France, and near us.

December 2nd.

Navvying, new reserve trenches in the wood.

December 3rd.

No. 12 Platoon relieved a platoon of the Essex Regiment. Wider and so more comfortable trenches. We have been supplied with goatskin coats, which we wear with the hair outwards, looking like Polar explorers. Foraged for green vegetables by crawling out to the field behind the trench. Shelled a little today.

December 4th.

The wind made fires and cooking very difficult. Some shells came round our corner;

beastly things, they shake you to bits; and one knocked down a whole section, 5 wounded, including Corporal Fender. 'Whizz-bangs' they call these field-gun shells. Whizz, bang, and a sheet of flame. Don't mind bullets, but can't help flinching at the whizz-bangs.

December 5th.

An awful day. Rained in torrents, trench became a muddy stream ankle deep, and the parapet kept falling down. We have no revetting material. Very difficult to cook breakfast, and we were tired and famished by the time we had our bacon fried, our tea made, and our biscuits and jam ready at 10 o'clock. Then whizz, bang! came the shells; showers of dirt all over us. We found a narrow deep spot and played at rabbits for a few minutes, seeking refuge with a rasher of bacon and a mug of tea in one fist and a biscuit and pot of jam in the other, desperately struggling to save our breakfast, so hardly won. There was no place to put it down.

We were wet through when relieved at 9 p.m. Pity our reliefs! How shall I ever get the mud off?

December 6th.

Sleeping; and getting the mud off.

December 7th.

Fatigues all day. Feeling very fit.

December 8th.

Back to the front line, taking over a stretch of our own, which shows the Staff trusts us. Proud to work with and relieve these splendid Tommies; most of them reservists. Told off with 3 men as H.Q. guard, so did not go up this time. Chance to dry my clothes; most cosy billet, plenty of fuel and food.

Awful mess on this paper is due to Stafford, who fell in a ditch on the way up, and was sent down to the guard-room (a brick barn with straw) to dry off.

Some papers came by post—just what I want here.

Made a very successful raisin rice pudding over a charcoal brazier. This is War; a straw-strewn barn, heaps of periodicals, a glowing brazier, puddings, and plenty.

Very wet outside. Poor wretches in the line!

December 11*th.*

Saw list of London Scottish casualties; many men I know.

December 12*th.*

More artistic cooking in the brazier. Bradfield has died of his wounds. Helped the Scout officer find billets for the battalion. I am in an estaminet with 24 others, very comfortable and warm. Lost my pack, with all my personal effects; appropriated a dead man's.

Moon, another old schoolfellow, hit on fatigue in the woods. Thirteen of ours killed so far. Everybody had parcels of food from their friends—we feed the village. The villagers love us. Mutton chops for supper.

Have only seen two Germans since leaving England. One was lying dead in a field; another I potted at. Funny war; you and the enemy dig holes in the ground 100 yards from each other, sit in them with your feet in water for weeks at a time, and get fat and lazy.

The Regulars are very complimentary about our efforts.

December 14*th.*

Still very comfortable at the estaminet—
'à Saint Mathia's. I am *persona grata* with
Monsieur and Madame, as I act as inter-
preter.

This afternoon Loudoun, Stafford, and I
procured a tub and some hot water, took it
up to the loft, and had a hot bath. Just
while we were drying, the Germans shelled
the village; never felt so naked.

December 15*th.*

More digging in the woods. Our guns
shelling.

At our estaminet, *Monsieur le patron* is big,
slow, good-humoured, and smokes a long
pipe, except when he takes it out to say
'Ouay' solemnly. Madame is large, kindly,
and has a maternal regard for me. Of the
two daughters, one is pretty, the other is not,
but both have voices like steam sirens. They
are nearly the best people in this village. The
little boy, Jules, son of a French soldier now
in hospital, is quite a character, phenomenally
sharp.

The shrapnel in the wood is troublesome;

have had some nearish shaves—and casualties mount up gradually—14 killed and 40 wounded.

I generally act as chief cook in this billet, being more or less expert at the game; we have some quite ambitious dishes.

December 19th.

No. 3 Company left in the morning to man reserve trenches in Tothill Fields. They are damp and sticky, and owing to the ease with which you strike water-level they are shallow. Very narrow, no room to pass, and no dug-outs. Archer and I rigged up a sort of bird-cage arrangement, with a roof and rear wall, with our waterproof sheet. Much rain. We placed our packs on the ground, and sat on them back to back and so kept moderately warm and safe. A few shells dropped into the mud behind among the trees, but not near enough to worry about. A mail arrived after dusk. Someone sent me the Bishop's address at the Guildhall, and I read it to those around, at their request.

Our guns were keeping up an incessant fire over our heads, and soon the machine-guns and rifles in front began. I believe the

idea was that the Regulars should drive out
the enemy from a corner of the wood they
still hold (I don't know where exactly) and
we were to be supporting troops ready to
move up if required.

After some hours' noise we were ordered
out and marched up to a point close behind
the front line. However, the other battalions
straightened out the line all right without the
help of us in reserve, though losses seem to
have been considerable. Our own casualties
were trifling: 1 killed and 5 wounded by a
chance shell.

We were uncomfortable enough, in light
attacking order, lying out in the mud and
wet and cold through the endless winter night,
but those who attacked in front must have had
an awful time. Floundering about in a
wilderness of holes made by our shells,
running up against barricades, surmounting
barbed wire, with machine-gun, rifle, and
shell-fire pouring on them, falling wounded
perhaps to drown in water-filled shell-holes,
or lying for hours and hours caked with mud,
and then a long jolting on stretchers along
slippery duckboards, poor devils!

December 20th.

Sunny all day. The Germans at all events
are as badly off as we are. I'm a mass of mud.

December 22nd.

Marched to Armentières, to a brewery on
the banks of the Lys, by the Pont de Nieppe,
to have hot baths. We are conducted to an
immense (and rather too airy) room where
we undress. Our uniforms are given up to
be baked, and we go below in our underclothes. These are given up; we scramble
into vats, about ten men to each vat, which is
filled with hot water. You get out, obtain
fresh underclothes, go upstairs and dress.
The company is allowed just one hour for
the job, so we have to hurry. Imagine a
large steaming vat, in which are ten heads
visible above the surface of the water, all
sitting in a ring with their feet to the centre;
presently one holds up a wee fish he has
found in the bath.

We are all snowed under with parcels.
There is a Brigade Order out about the show
on the 19th. In it we read that it was supposed to pin German troops to this front to
prevent them from fighting the Russians.

On the other hand, the official communiqué (known as Comic Cuts) dismisses the whole thing in two lines. Can't help thinking Comic Cuts has a better sense of values.

December 23rd.

We are going up to the line tonight. We subscribed for presents for Monsieur and Madame and the young ones; gave them three cheers and musical honours, to their astonishment and delight. The *patron* became quite animated, he said 'Vivent les Anglais' a great many times.

December 24th.

In a breastwork, and quite comfortable— ground too waterlogged for a trench—a barricade of sand-bags and earth about $3\frac{1}{2}$ feet high, and a shrapnel-proof roof of logs, planks, and earth; with another barricade behind to guard against back-bursts.

Fatigues (log-rolling) from 9 to 2.30. I was told off (with three men) for H.Q. guard again. Bright moon, and freezing hard; fell over three times on the corduroy path on the way down.

G

December 25th, Christmas Day.

The guard-room is a small shed with dirty straw, which we share with a machine-gun section of the Regulars. These cheerful souls are this quiet morning engaged in picking lice out of the seams of their clothing.

For dinner we warmed two tins of Maconochie (M. and V. ration) and some Christmas pudding sent from home, with biscuits, butter, jam, and coffee.

Life is one great battle with water and mud. The paths are neatly labelled with names reminiscent of home, 'Piccadilly Circus', for example. One ramshackle hut has a notice board outside, 'SIC TRANSIT GLORIA MUNDI'.

Even the German shells and our axes have not yet spoilt the beauty of these great woods. In spring they must be lovely. Last year's nests still swing on the rustling twigs; and robins, wrens, and chaffinches chirrup still around. They resound to the blows of hammer and axe, to the tramp of feet, shouts and whistle and song, or to the scream and crash of a shell; but when the rare gleam of winter sunshine strays along the rides, one cannot help thinking of the high woods of home.

Last night was a cheerful one in the trenches and barricades. We all made merry with carols, mouth-organs and popular songs. The Germans also made a rare noise, and all along the lines there was cheering and singing.

Today a number of our fellows and the Germans have been chatting between the lines, swapping cigarettes, and so on.

The Regulars H.Q. have sent out to us of the guard some hot roast beef, potatoes, fruit, and beer.

I joined the company at 8 p.m. at the breastwork, curled up round the brazier, and slept for a few hours. Followed long hours of fatigues (sand-bags to the firing line) and then the company took over the front line.

December 26th.

Extraordinary as it may seem, it is a firing-line in name only. In the trenches held by our brigade at all events there has been a truce since Christmas Day. As I write now some of the British are out talking to the Germans in the No-Man's Land between our trenches, swopping souvenirs and tobacco, and becoming good friends.

Yesterday there were hundreds and hundreds of both sides, officers and men, in between the lines. We carried over some German dead and helped to bury them. Their officer read some prayers and thanked (in English) 'his English friends' for bringing them over. Lots of them speak English. One man said he was a hairdresser in the Strand, and another was a London hotel waiter.

These trenches are fairly good, and with no firing going on, we are having an easy time. The enemy here are Saxons. We can hear firing going on, away on the flanks.

December 28th.

At present I am in what is left of a house. Except for a few beams (many broken) nothing is left of the roof. A guard lives in the cellar, while another man and I are snipers upstairs, but owing to the truce there is nothing to do. We can see all the fraternizing going on. A captain and one subaltern of our company are temporarily attached to a company of a Regular battalion, who lost all their officers in the affair of the 19th.

December 30th.

Worked all evening, bringing up supplies and then took over. Fine clear night after the rain, but cold. The goatskins keep us warm except for our feet, which get wet right away and then remain wet for days till we get back to billets.

Truce still continues; most amazing. Starting with the 'peace and good will' idea on Christmas Day, it was found so mutually pleasant and convenient that neither side, though keeping close watch, fires a shot. The other day the German C.O. expected a visit from a general, and said he would be opening fire between 11 and 12, and we had better keep our heads down.

We are making good use of the 'peace', but no doubt the Germans are working hard too.

December 31st.

The other day a big German stood up on the parapet, lighted his pipe and shouted, 'Hallo, Rifles, how are you this morning?' and one night they called out, 'Now then, Corporal Anderson, what about that listening patrol?' I suppose they had overheard this remark the night before.

1915

1915

January 1st.

WE sang 'Auld Lang Syne' and 'God save the King' to bring the New Year in, but we were too sleepy to keep it up. Dirty weather.

January 6th.

Back in billets. Benson, three others and myself are in a cottage in 'Plugstreet'.

At the estaminet today there were four Gordon Highlanders sitting round a table, all a little drunk, and solemnly singing some slow and plaintive air. One had a clear strong tenor, and the others filled up with a deeper harmony. They sang 'Ye Banks and Braes' right through, and sang it jolly well. Made Adrienne stare.

The Tommies and Jocks are really splendid. Some of them rough, some not; but all good stuff.

On the night of the attack on the 19th of

December, after it was over, we were still standing by (i.e. sitting in the marshy woods in the rain) and the men who had actually gone over the top came singing back along the duck-boards. They had lost heavily, been wet through, and nearly smothered in mud for hours and hours, and must have been tired out, but they strode along full of go, with never a grumble, and with many a cheery word for us; and with a grim humour that rather appealed to me one man with a fine voice was singing as he tramped back the well-known air, 'O for the wings, for the wings of a dove,—far away, far away would I rove'. They are wonderful.

One of the battalions in our brigade has a piper. They say some parts of the pipes are historic, they were used 100 years ago in Belgium in the Waterloo campaign.

January 8th.

Had an interesting walk today with Walter Potts and Jones. We walked up to the Crucifix at Le Gheer, to collect some odds and ends of German equipment as souvenirs. The enemy started to shell one of the battalion head-quarters as we passed along the road, and I took a snapshot of a big black shell bursting just by the barns and throwing up the earth all around, while the men were streaming out. (The truce has collapsed at last.) They put over some nasty-looking yellow shrapnel too. We got up unseen in a slight mist and secured some souvenirs; 'pork pie' caps, pouches, etc.

Am putting on weight, with fattening foods!

We are settling down to a steady routine, trenches, reserve, and village billets, with fatigues all the time of course; rather a comfortable existence for active service, as things are rather quiet.

It is an appalling job filling sand-bags with wet mud. It sticks on the spade, on your clothes, and does anything but slide into the sack.

January 9th.

We have gone back a century or two, and are using hand-grenades made out of the 1-lb. jam-tins, also rifle-grenades.

January 10th.

Company Church Parade in a school-room (we are in billets). Someone discovered a piano, and while waiting for the padre started playing as a voluntary Edward German's dances from 'Nell Gwynn'.

January 14th.

We no longer relieve companies of the other battalions, but have a battalion section of trench of our own to have and to hold, for better for worse, etc. When we took it over it was in a terrible state, but with the help of some pumps the water has been checked. One man got stuck up to the waist and was only got out with difficulty. We spend our time pumping, revetting, building up the parapet, baling, making bivouac shelters, putting down planks for flooring, sentry duty, cooking, eating, and sleeping. We have a good supply of coke (wet) and charcoal for braziers. Weather vile.

Two killed this journey, one being Tommy Samson, who was in my tent at Bisley and Crowborough. He and some others were trying to repair a dangerous exposed place, and he moved incautiously across the opening. A sniper's bullet zipped through and a piece of his lung fell out of his back. He died in about an hour.

Billeted this time in a factory at Armen-

tières. Another hot bath in the brewery.
About 12 or 14 of us were sitting round in a
vat, up to our necks, and half hidden in
steam, singing 'Drake Goes West' at the top
of our voices, when the R.A.M.C. man
shouted 'Time's Up!' and turned the cold
water hose on us, and we flung ourselves out
in heaps. Then, while we dried ourselves,
we watched the next vat. We could not see
the occupants from below, but they were
parodying a speech made at a hilarious dinner
when we were at Bisley:

'Gentlemen of the Rifles,'—(hooray)—'we are assembled
together this morning'—(hooray)———

'Come on, get out of it!' breaks in the
R.A.M.C., plying the hose, and immediately
a dozen naked forms emerge, and clamber over,
the hindmost getting most of the cold water.

I overheard the following the other night.
A number of our boys were engaged in
carrying sand-bags up to the front line. It
is very hard work; and a Tommy, watching
the endless procession, remarked in an amazed
tone to his mate, 'These 'ere Territorial
blokes MAKES A BLOOMIN' 'OBBY of this kind
of thing'!

Pat fell in a ditch in the dark and fractured his leg.

A team from Support Farm today beat the R.A.M.C. by 6 goals to 3. Sometimes the ball would plump into a shell-hole with a crash of breaking ice.

January 15th.

At Armentières there is a cinema and Divisional Follies. The turns are provided by talent among the troops. Good fun, but I wish I could hear some good music.

Our food, equipment, and organization are the amazement of the natives. They think we are all millionaires, and call us the 'Gentlemen of the Black Buttons'.

Firle, Benson and I had an excellent little dinner at the Hotel de France.

January 16th.

Hurricane of wind and rain. Our platoon is in support. 'At present we are staying on a farm' as Bairnsfather has it. A somewhat battered building, which we have fortified. We have to keep in by day, and by night stray bullets fly around.

January 18*th.*

This afternoon 3 men sitting round the fire
got up a spur-of-the-moment street-corner
agitator's meeting, with interruptions. They
kept it up for about an hour, to our great
amusement. It was all about our Sand-bag
Factory Federation, and the question of
soldiers' rum, and rubber boots.

January 20*th.*

Another bath. Amusing to watch the
fellows coming along with their new underclothing on. Such queer colour schemes of
scarlet, blue, and salmon-pink, and often
quaint misfits. Then we gather with upturned patient faces round a platform, awaiting our trousers from the ovens, where they
have been baked to destroy any unwelcome
visitors that may be lurking in the seams.
Rubber gum-boots are issued for trench wear.
We are using periscopes in the trenches.

January 26*th.*

Had some successful sniping through steel
plates, and kept down the German fire quite
a lot. No. 11 Platoon marched back along
the road singing on relief; but we stepped it

out to a mouth-organ! Reinforcements arrived from the 2nd Battalion. Have cut six inches off the bottom of my greatcoat to prevent it trailing in the mud.

Sometimes at night an unaccountable outburst of firing is heard far away in the north: it runs like a wind down the trenches, getting louder and louder: we stand to, and pour rapid fire into No-Man's Land. It slackens, and we stand down, and hear it travelling down south. They call it a 'wind-up', and 'getting the wind up' is becoming quite a regular term for a panic. Talking of slang, the Tommies' name for England is 'Blighty'. This puzzled me for a bit, till I remembered one of Kipling's stories in which *'Belait'* occurs as a Hindustanee word for Europe. I suppose they brought it from India. And 'buckshee', meaning free or gratuitous, is, I suppose, the same as 'baksheesh'.

January 27th.

Armentières. A short run before breakfast, and a route march afterwards. Divisional Follies again—a very good Pierrot programme, soldier men and two French girls, with lighting effects from an A.S.C. lorry head-light.

Our billet is on a main road, and all day
long there is a stream of traffic of all kinds.
Lumbering queer-shaped carts, fast motor-
lorries, with canvas tilts daubed like futurist
paintings, long strings of led horses, mounted
officers, officers on motor-cycles or in cars,
columns of infantry, artillery, Red Cross
ambulances—simply to sit and look at it is
full of interest.

January 28th.

Visited the great church of Armentières
today, early Gothic in style, and richly and
splendidly decorated within, beautiful oak
carving and panelling, glowing stained glass,
rare marbles, and nothing specious or tawdry,
such as one often sees in the Continental
churches. An exquisite statue of Joan of Arc,
sweet inspired expression. If I were a Frenchman in these days, I would be always dropping
in to get courage and hope from that statue.

Saw a man threshing with a flail.

A characteristic of this landscape are the
heaps of stacked earthed beets, and the
chimneys of sugar factories; also bundles of
tobacco leaves hanging up to dry in sheds.

H

February 1st.

Fingerless gloves from Toronto have been issued, also mackintosh capes. Young Pope wounded. Have been sketching in the woods with Linden.

February 2nd.

Concert in 'Plugstreet'. One of our men is baritone soloist at St. Peter's, Eaton Square. He sang tonight—great success—jolly good concert. We had the piper too.

February 3rd.

In the front line again. Our trench is really luxurious, and we are having an easy time these days, with comfortable weather-proof dug-outs, plenty of food and clothes, and with reasonable care not much chance of getting hurt, at present.

Support Farm sends us hot soup at night in biscuit tins packed in straw.

February 4th.

P. is mortally wounded. Weather cold but dry. We rub our feet with whale oil before coming up the line. Exactly 3 months since we landed at Le Havre.

February 6th.

Hear that Corporal Small is dead of gastritis—a real loss. Had a very close shave from a bullet that penetrated a sand-bag. Effected the necessary repairs.

Linden and I made some panorama sketches of the enemy position through periscopes.

February 8th.

I have just come across these lines by A. E., which I like, because the stars are your only companions on sentry duty in the trenches; and they seem filled with majesty and peace, as does the sunrise too.

> 'Ah, no, the circle of the heavenly ones,
> That ring of burning, grave, inflexible powers,
> Array in harmony amid the deep
> The shining legionaries of the suns,
> That through the day from dawn to twilight keep
> The peace of heaven, and have no feuds like ours.
>
> The morning stars their labours of the dawn
> Close at the advent of the solar kings,
> And these with joy their sceptres yield withdrawn
> When the still evening stars begin their reign,
> AND TWILIGHT TIME IS THRILLED WITH HOMING WINGS
> TO THE ALL-FATHER BEING TURNED AGAIN.'

February 9th.

Commanding officer's inspection. They are very properly now getting very particular about our smart clean turn-out when in billets. The beards and the mud have to come off at once.

February 11th.

At Mountain Gun Farm. The guard-room (I am corporal of the guard) is a little brick hut about 8 feet square, luckily with the window side away from the enemy. There is a log fire burning in the open hearth, a sentry stands outside the window, and the two others are sleeping beside me on the straw. Bullets whirl by us into the farm courtyard, and now and then whop against the walls, but it is very snug inside.

February 18th.

It is impossible to live through a dreary winter in this God-forsaken country without feeling very sorry for the wretched inhabitants. It is sad to see the smashed and blackened ruin of what was once a prosperous neat little farm, and to think of what has happened to the hard-working peasant folk.

Some of the farms we occupy in support line are within a few hundred yards of the front line, and in many cases the people still cling desperately to what is left. There are civilian folk still at Mountain Gun Farm.

At home one abuses the enemy, and draws insulting caricatures. How tired I am of grotesque Kaisers! Out here, one can respect a brave, skilful, and resourceful enemy. They have people they love at home, they too have to endure mud, rain and steel.

February 16th.

Glorious day, warm sun. It is funny to sit here quietly chatting and reading with a peaceful view behind over field and wood, when if you move two feet you are as good as dead. A pied wagtail keeps running about in front, heedless of the cracking bullets.

Being Shrove Tuesday we made pancakes! We brought up eggs yesterday, and Nestlé's milk.

February 17th.

Last night I was in charge of a listening patrol in front. I held a piece of string, the other end of which was in the hand of the sergeant. After about two hours' boredom one of those 'wind-ups' that start Heaven knows how began, and the whole place was alive with whistling, crackling bullets and bright with soaring lights. The sergeant jerked the string, and we scrambled back safely through the wire, hurling ourselves desperately towards the row of staring faces lining the trench white in the glare of the lights; but nothing came of it all.

Yesterday I saw a man eating soup with a fork. He had made it with two packets of pea flour, three Oxo cubes, a pint of water, some bread crumbs, and a few lumps of mud from the parapet contributed by the German riflemen.

February 18th.

Now watching a ruined convent behind the trench being shelled. When a shell hits the building dense clouds of pink dust and black smoke blow away.

February 19th.

Armentières. This morning the Major told me I am to go to the Base shortly to the Cadet School to be trained for a commission.

In the British Army zone a sort of bastard neutral language is springing up, neither French nor English, but 'odds and ends and leavings of the same', helped out with plentiful shrugs and gestures.

February 21st.

Third draft arrived.

February 22nd.

Doing a good deal of sketching on odd bits of paper and note-books in spare moments. Have already sent some home; hope they won't be censored.

February 23rd.

Shell in the pigsty next to No. 11 Platoon's quarters; killed both pigs.

February 26th.

The C.O. has got the C.M.G. and is acting brigadier. Tonight we had a company concert in 'Plugstreet'. Barton sang gloriously, and one of the Jocks sang 'Roaming in the Gloaming' very well. I sang two songs.

February 27th.

The turn of the year is coming. Brown catkins and faint green buds in the woods.

February 28th.

We have dug out of the parapet a German rifle which we have cleaned and oiled, and used against them; there is some German ammunition about. We potted through the steel loophole plate at their loopholes.

Left the trenches on my way to the Base. Prayed I would not 'stop one' on the way down!

March 1st.

Am in a comfortably furnished room eating a jolly good cooked meal, and only about a mile from the front line. The battalion now has the short regular rifle. Am held up for 2 or 3 days.

March 4th.

Truly sorry to leave the regiment; they are a splendid crowd.

March 5th.

Having already said good-bye in the trenches, I tried to slip out quietly this morning, but had a crowd to see me off all the same.

I met 8 others from the battalion at

Divisional H.Q. We had a ride in a motor-lorry to Bailleul. I felt, sitting on a box beside the driver, just as if I were back at school again, and playing an away match.

March 6th.

Great scrubbing of floors, benches, tables, etc., of our lecture-rooms.

March 7th.

The School is a large white house in the Rue de Musée, Bailleul. We have to parade as spotless as in peace time, no easy job with an equipment fresh from a winter in the trenches. This is a four-weeks' course of drill, field work, map-reading, M.G. work, elementary surveying, billeting, trench-fighting, etc.

March 9th.

Our class (or division as it is called) walked up independently in groups to the top of Mont Noir, from which there is a really magnificent view all over Western Flanders. From a windmill on the summit one can see a score of places historic in old wars and already historic in this. We spent some hours up there, map-reading, taking bearings, lunching at a tiny estaminet, and returning to our 5 o'clock dinner.

The country round here is more varied and hilly, and is very little knocked about by shell fire; the war is hardly noticeable.

March 13*th.*

Practised making rafts and floating across a pool, much as prehistoric man must have done.

After lunch there was the usual Saturday-afternoon scrub. We arm ourselves with scrubbing-brushes, soap, and basins, slop dirty water on the floor, swish it about, and then painfully mop it up with sacking. Then some blunderer comes in with muddy boots. When he has retired hurt, someone else steps on the rim of the basin; so more dirty water floods the floor. Then there are the forms, tables, and cupboards; oh, it is a game! The ridge of hills—Mont Noir, Mont des Cats, Mont Kemmel—is really pretty; clean little farms and cottages on the lower slopes, precipitous sandpits, and tall beeches on the steep hill-sides. It is a beautiful warm spring afternoon, though misty; and the robins, thrushes, and tits are nesting, and singing as if they were English. Only there are no primroses, nor daffodils to 'take the winds of March with beauty', nor any sign of blue-bells. *Dulce domum, O sodales.*

March 14th.

Superb view from the summit of the Mont des Cats. There is a great Trappist monastery on it (almost undamaged) with a few old monks, and British cavalry, living in the place.

March 15th.

Tomorrow we go up to the front line for 24 hours to write a report. Told today that leave was stopped.

> 'Things like this you know must be
> After a famous victory.'
> (NEUVE CHAPELLE!)

March 16th.

In the trenches near Messines Ridge, with the 1st East Surreys (C Company). A weary march up over long miles of *pavé*. I was walking about outside the trench till 2 a.m. Captain Huth was most kind and helpful. I mess with him and his subaltern, and share a dug-out with the platoon sergeant,

Brown, a splendid chap. Spent the morning making maps, plans, and reports on the position. Fine and warm day. The moment it is dark enough to venture out, everything and everybody wakes up. Visiting officers, N.C.O.'s, ration parties, sanitary parties, patrols, working parties, all buzz round; the trench takes on fresh life, additional sentries are posted, and now the snipers begin to get busy as the Verey lights soar up to spill in pools of radiance.

I was held up when leaving, missed the last lorries, and had to tramp the whole 9 miles back to Bailleul over villainous *pavé*, arriving tired and sleepy.

March 19th.

Had a hot bath in the town, the best since the hotel at Crowborough.

March 20th.

Cross-country compass march. I fell into a ditch, icy water up to my waist.

March 22nd.

Looked in at the big church. A service on, Benediction, I suppose. Litanies, and

beautiful chants—the *O Salutaris.* Went to
church myself last Sunday.

March 23rd.

Wonderful sky effect about 6 o'clock.
All the east a gorgeous rose colour, with a
rainbow shining through it. The square was
filled with little groups staring at it.

March 25th.

Our division was given a company of dis-
gusted Artists' Riflemen to drill in the wind
and the rain.

In the afternoon we drilled some Bryant
and May's matches on the table!

Went to a cottage where they make lace
by hand, and spent a few francs.

March 28th, Sunday.

Cold, but gloriously fine. In the afternoon walked over about 8 miles to 'Plugstreet' to see the boys. The platoon was in
billets, and I had tea with them. Linden
and Holly walked along with me some
distance, and at the Transport billets in
Romarin picked up Bertie Cameron, who
came along for a mile or so. I enjoyed my

visit very much; I swear no Territorial regiment touches them.

March 31*st*.

We received destructive criticism of our field operations. I think perhaps that months of discomfort and navvying work has not exactly sharpened us, and that this school has shaken us together a lot. General Baden-Powell paid us a visit this morning during the lecture. After he had gone we each in turn had to give brief impromptu lectures to the others on subjects announced then and there. My subject was 'Contours'.

Revolver competition this afternoon. The Bishop of London held a service in the town at 6 o'clock. He seemed tired out.

April 2*nd*.

Had a succession of fine days. Tonight a lecture by Captain Johnstone, V.C., on Sub-terranean Warfare.

Glorious hot bath tonight in the School. You fill a copper by means of a bucket and a pump, kindle a fire, ladle the hot water into the bath, and then take your tub. All rather complicated, as you have to empty the bath with a bucket (flinging the contents into the road), refill the copper and stoke the fire for the next man.

This morning Captain Green left for home leave. He has taught us a lot in his caustic way.

Major Currie, the commandant, gave us a lecture today. He has been with the 13th Brigade, consisting of the K.O.S.B., K.O.Y.L.I., Duke of Wellington's Regiment, and the Buffs, as Brigade Major, since the beginning. He told us how they held the canal at Mons, and found that the French were not there, but that three and a half German Army Corps were; and how they fell back at length to Wasmes, where the Duke of Wellington's Regiment were almost destroyed as a unit; and then the great story of Le Cateau.

Here they fought from 8 in the morning till 4 in the afternoon, until but shattered remnants of these famous regiments were left, against overwhelming masses of Germans, and the most appalling concentration of artillery fire ever known. Major Currie is a soldierly type of man, and not in the least given to 'telling the tale'; but he faltered once or twice as if he did not know how to find words to tell the moving story of how the guns were served at Le Cateau. All day long the gunners worked like heroes, firing incessantly. He was behind one of the three field batteries. At first above the din he kept hearing the six guns speak; again and again. Later five guns only spoke, then four; three; then he heard but two; till one gun only was left, still heroically served by a tiny handful. At last came the end; and Major Currie merely took the duster and wiped the battery off his sketch-map on the board. Out of 3 batteries of 18 guns only 2 guns were saved.

The infantry passed the 60-pounder battery in their retreat. Their officer was having the time of his life, causing immense execution among the dense masses of the enemy, and they had great difficulty in getting him away.

Today we have heard a story seldom told before, and which very few in England have heard. There has never been anything like it in history before, a rear-guard fight against such overwhelming odds, waged with such magnificent courage. The old B.E.F. was, through no fault of its own, sacrificed, but its discipline and tenacity saved France and saved Europe.

After dinner walked with a friend up to Mont Noir.

April 4th, Easter Sunday.

Territorials are out here in tens of thousands, fine troops too. The authorities have wisely, though tardily, realized the value of bands, and so now one regiment in each brigade brings its band out. This afternoon the Sherwood Foresters (T.F.) played selections from 'The Gondoliers' in the square.

Have been doing some sketching. After tea the Commandant finished his lecture of the previous day by giving a brief sketch of the great retreat to the south of Paris, and the subsequent *volte-face* and pursuit of the Germans to the Aisne.

There are three points to notice in this retreat from Mons—(1) Our right was always uncovered, owing to the French being always expected, and never there; (2) the magnificent discipline of the highly trained British Regular troops, who calmly endured what no other army has ever had to do before in the way of artillery fire; (3) the quality of the German troops.

I

Their numbers were enormous, their guns were well-handled, but the infantry lacked push and *élan*. Several times they should have wiped us out completely, but they were too slow, and we got away.

April 5th.

Rode in a 'General' motor-bus to St. Omer, and dumped our few belongings at the same old barracks (Solferino) I was in before, last November. Here I learnt that I have been posted to the 2nd Battalion of a famous Highland regiment with Newman of the London Scottish. He and I had a civilized dinner at the Hotel de France.

April 7th.

Boulogne at 7.15 a.m. Embarked on the 'Onward', leaving at 10. Bright and sunny, but half a westerly gale blowing, so it was pretty rough. It was fine to see the sunbows leaping overside with the spray.

Here I am bowling through Kent, home at last, though only till Sunday, and today's Wednesday!

April 7th–11th.

HAPPY DAYS!

April 12*th.*

After landing at Boulogne, Newman and I drove to the Hotel Meurice, where we had an excellent dinner. We boarded our train at 8.15, and at 6.15 next morning reached Vlamertinghe, the rail-head, and a poor sort of village. We breakfasted at a rough esta-minet off gritty bread, boiled eggs and coffee, and went by bus into Ypres.

The battalion is in the line at present, but we found the Quartermaster. The town is an extraordinary sight. It is shelled most days, and is gradually being battered to pieces.

April 13*th,* 12.30 *a.m.*

Am sitting in my dug-out, writing by candle-light, after tramping round all the night. Two nights ago in a London theatre, now commanding 57 men in action.

We had a second breakfast before coming up, in a house well appointed and furnished, but with all the glass broken, and windows stuffed with sacking.

1.15 *p.m.* Am commanding the support platoon of our company, which is in the first trench. We are living in dug-outs in Sanc-tuary Wood. They were lately occupied by the French, and were left in a filthy state; no attempt at sanitation or cleanliness, in fact they looked as if they had been used as latrines. We have had a busy time cleaning them out.

The Frenchmen may be brave soldiers, but their ideas of health and decency are not ours.

The woods are shelled a good deal, but the robins and thrushes sing and nest, as if all was right with the world. After all, we get callous, why shouldn't they? At night we fetch rations for the front line, and do any other fatigues that are necessary, but do nothing in particular during the day time. We cannot light fires, as the smoke would draw shell-fire. I shall buy a spirit stove. In the first trench one can cook as much as one likes, because the enemy knows exactly where that is, and a little smoke gives nothing away.

My brother officers seem a splendid lot. The Colonel is a tall, well-built man, with a ruddy face, sandy moustache, a cheery smile, twinkling blue eyes, and a nearly bald head, on which he wears a ridiculous blue cap, with a red toorie on top. The Adjutant is affectionately known as Big Mac.

Inspected my platoon's rifles this morning. Some of them thought I was new to the game, and that anything would do for me. But they were wrong; I have heard all the excuses before!

April 14th.

Got my sergeant to show me the way up to the first trench; only a very little way, but the position is so exposed that by day one has to be very canny, and it takes time.

April 15th.

Worked all day at making a sketch through a periscope of the enemy position as seen from our battalion front. Glorious day, clear hot sun. These woods are quite beautiful in the grouping of the trees, which are mostly pine, with a sprinkling of beech. There is also a lake, and a château, nicknamed Stirling Castle. But the trees are rent and cruelly torn, the sandy earth is honeycombed with trenches and dug-outs, and hasty nameless graves are scattered here and there. Today I came upon the bodies of three horses, one blown in half, evidently killed by the same shell weeks ago, that our French friends had never troubled to bury, so we had to do it. The front line is only 30 yards from the enemy in some places, and they potted at my periscope every time I put it up, sending showers of earth down my neck.

What a mix-up things are! I am sitting in my dug-out this evening eagerly discussing over a mug of tea poets and poems with a brother officer, when he is called away about some ammunition for his machine-gun. I pick up a book, and being in the middle of a fairy-like sonnet, am sent for about a little matter of bombs! Trouble expected.

April 16th.

No trouble occurred, to the deep disgust of our men, who had made all things ready, and were praying that the Germans would come to supper.

As I remarked before, things are queerly mixed. One picks up a man with his brains blown out (they *will* not keep their dear silly heads down!) and five minutes after we have forgotten the pitiful sight, and are laughing over some jest. The particular jest here was a 'model' of H.M.S. 'Lion' that the men were floating about in the communication trench (this is 50 yards from the Boches). It was made from a piece of corky bark from a big pine. The gun turrets and funnels were also fashioned from the bark, and she had four guns (cartridge cases) for'ard and four aft.

Some of the lads are incredibly careless. I came across one standing on the top hauling up a sand-bag on to the parapet. He was in full view of the enemy, 50 yards away, only mercifully no one opposite happened to be looking at the moment. My vigorous language scared him into leaping down quickly, or he would have been shot right enough.

Awfully dark tonight, and it made reliefs difficult. I fell in a ditch as usual, and walked right into a horse's nose. Don't know who was most surprised.

Queer to see a long file of men laden with stores for the front line suddenly lit up out of the blackness by the flash of a shell bursting close by, and swaying as one man towards the white clay walls of the ruined cottages of Hooge.

The stink of the explosive is in my nostrils yet. Another smell that I shall remember till I die, whether that be soon or late, is that of chloride of lime, which is very useful to drown other smells, such as that of putrefying remnants of bodies, which you sometimes find in the trench. And they put chloride of lime into the water, which often comes up in petrol cans. Imagine the tea made with such water! It has an unforgettable taste.

We returned through the Menin Gate, reaching billets in Ypres at 1 a.m. I saw the men in, had a meal, and turned in at 2.

April 17th.

Breakfasted at 11. My bedroom is a large apartment with a fine oak bedstead, wardrobe, and dressing table. Our company officers' mess-room is large, well furnished, with an excellent piano, and we sing and play and thoroughly enjoy our rest. The house is empty, and belongs to a Belgian major now on service; we are much obliged to him.

Last night, or to be more accurate, this morning, I took off my boots for the first time since Sunday morning, when I put them on at home.

April 18th.

Tremendous artillery fire all night. There is plenty of ventilation. The room is well

furnished, but the whole front has fallen out
and is open to the street. As the houses
opposite are quite ruined and deserted one is
not overlooked. Business as usual, where
possible, is the citizens' motto; and the
Grand Place is thronged with peasant women
selling produce at their stalls, and the streets
are alive with uniforms from England, Scotland, Ireland, and Wales, France, Belgium,
and North Africa, and last, but not least,
Canada, good husky men.

Church Parade was in a Belgian barrack-
room. The old Presbyterian padre had a
hard job to make himself heard in the sunlit,
shell-scarred room, because troops were marching back from the trenches, with songs and
mouth-organs, and every now and then the
place would be filled with the roar of ammunition columns over the *pavé*, or the tramp of
feet.

Yesterday I received a present of a writing-
case and chocolate from an unknown donor,
dated March some time, in the north of
Scotland; evidently a soldier, for he has
written a card: 'Entrenched in snow. Are
ye cauld with the kilt? For I'm kilt with the
cauld.'

Tonight C Company (that's us, the officers) invited some other fellows round, including a 'musical marvel'. We kept things going all evening, with Gilbert and Sullivan songs, songs I had with me, and others we remembered—a most cheery time. We made a rare noise!

April 19th.

Rather more shells this morning than usual in the town. Getting somewhat unhealthy. The C.O. sent for me this morning, and read me a letter from the Divisional General, thanking me and congratulating me on my very useful work (the panorama trench sketch). So that's not bad for a start!

April 20th.

Decidedly this place is becoming a warm corner; many casualties from shell-fire.

It is laughable, when you come to think of it, three men seated round a table in a large well-furnished room, breaking off their conversation, and listening, with hands gripping the table, to the *whoo—oo* of a shell as it comes nearer and nearer, bracing themselves for the crash.

Glad I'm not much cursed with nerves, as this place does not equal Bournemouth as a rest cure. They send H.E. here, huge fellows; horrid crashes, and showers of falling masonry, while we stand on the ground floor, hoping one won't hit our house. This *is* a life!

A man has sought refuge in our house, his nerves all gone. He sobbed and moaned a little as each one came.

The glorious Cloth Hall and the Cathedral are fast going to pieces.

Later. We have packed up and 'quitted', as our Canadian friends say, and at present the battalion is sitting on the high banks of the canal in the sun, very pleasant, and watching the big shells burst in the town a mile away. We are well out of it, for these are monsters, make a noise like a railway train as they lumber through the air, and burst with a terrifying crash and volumes of black smoke. This is a quiet sunny spot, the broad canal bordered with tall trees and on either side steep banks and meadows covered with cowslips.

We bivouacked here, very cold, and at 3.30 a.m. started for Ypres.

April 21*st*.

Day broke as we emerged from the city, though it was midday before we reached our destination about 2 miles out, as we halted twice in dug-outs, and behind embankments. We picked our way along a railway cutting, littered with the foul débris of a battle-field, rags and broken equipment strewn over the rusting rails. We were under shell-fire the whole time, especially the last bit, before we reached a larch plantation on the slope of a hill south of Zillebeke, known on the map as Hill 60.

All the way the landscape seemed dead, the solitude uncanny. There was a death-like silence over all, broken only by the whine and crash of a shell every minute or so.

April 25*th*.

Am now in the Casualty Clearing Station, a bare red brick building in Poperinghe, feeling rather shivery and empty, wounded, but not badly, by a whizz-bang, in the right leg.

I have been on Hill 60 with the battalion, which was lent by the Division to reinforce the 5th Brigade, for four days. We had no actual attack to repel, for the enemy seems to have been busy on our flank, but we have had a bad time with shells and trench mortars. The trench mortar is a horrible engine; the concussion of the shell is terrific; it blows your heavy muddy kilt about your thighs even when bursting a long distance out of harm's way, and whole stretches of trench may be blown in by it. One thing, you hear the faint thud of the discharge, look up, see it coming, whirling and twisting in the air, and scuttle along the trench away from it. But this gets on your nerves after a while; it is so tiring dodging up and down the trench like that.

Many good officers, N.C.O.'s and men have gone west.

Etched in my brain is the picture of one of our officers lying dead, sprawling on his back, head down, mouth open, eyes staring in the middle of what was once a section of trench, now a jumble of upturned earth and ruptured sand-bags; a pitiful sight.

One morning I had a mug of tea and a biscuit and jam, and was just going to begin breakfast when I was seized with a momentary nausea, followed by a fit of coughing. My eyes began to smart and run. I walked along and found my men coughing and crying too. 'Whatever is the matter with us all?' said I. 'It's the gahss, sir-r!' replied a corporal. GAS! Something new in war. However, it passed off.

All one night my platoon was busy digging, extending our section of trench. I was awake all night, and at daybreak fell asleep on the floor of the trench with all my men save a few sentries. I suddenly woke in the sunlight to see the C.O. with his twinkling eyes and his ridiculous cap looking down on me, leaning on his stick. 'Don't get up, my boy, don't get up,' said he, as I struggled to rise. 'I've just come to see how you've been getting on,' and he picked his way over the sprawling men.

We were being relieved early this (Sunday) morning. I was leading my platoon along a communication trench down the hill. Sergeant Sinclair was next to me, and Platoon Sergeant Macdonald, a little lithe dark sibilant Highlander, brought up the rear. At the bottom of the hill the trench ceased, and apparently we were seen all along (that is the worst of this salient) for whizz-bangs were scattered along it.

As the trench was really a moving river of mud, when the men ducked down to avoid the shell splinters they were almost engulfed in slime, which clung round their clothing, and made it difficult to drag one limb after another. Sinclair and I and another man emerged, and before we could succeed in making a dash for cover near by, we were knocked over by a shell. Sinclair was badly hit in the head, and I greatly fear he is done for. My leg was useless, so I crawled a few yards to the cover of a bank, sent the other man running across where the going was fairly good to report to battalion head-quarters, and tried to get the men to come out one by one and dash over to me. But the noise of the rain and the shells drowned my voice, though I did not want the men to remain in the mud, as their morale would be ruined, and they would be unable to walk if they stayed there; indeed many could only just crawl.

So I sat there shouting to them to come out, and gradually one or two began to come across on their hands and knees.

Just then, my friend Arthur (to whom I shall ever be grateful) and one or two other officers came along, and helped me up. Their arrival was greeted by a shell, which made me fall down again, but harmed no one. But the shelling then ceased, and we, or rather they, got the men, including the casualties, together somehow, and with their support I hobbled back.

I was in a pretty mess from mud and rain, and was inoculated for tetanus and well rubbed with iodine on the leg. Sat beside the driver of an ambulance van to Pop. from just outside Ypres. He disliked the journey as much as I did; one feels, and is, so overlooked in this region, and there was still more desultory shelling going on. Passed the Rifles on their way up, and waved to many of the boys. Good luck to them! I seem to have caught a slight chill with catarrh, the latter perhaps due to the whiff of gas we got on the Hill.

April 27th.

Hospital train, and now a comfortable hospital in Boulogne, with some dear sisters in charge.

Noon. Suddenly packed off to the steamer for home, labelled like a piece of luggage. Good old Dover!

In a cubicle at Guy's Hospital; luxurious;
everybody most kind.

April 28th.

The Jocks are rather different in style to
the English Tommies. There is not so much
noisy laughter, they are more serious, and
not so given to flippancy as are the English
of the South. Tommy is always talking, and
always trying manfully to be funny, often
successfully. Jock is more silent, and doesn't
bubble over at you. I suppose when it
comes to fighting one is just as good as the
other.

April 29th.

Throat too bad to take an anæsthetic, so
did not go to the operating theatre.

It was very surprising to observe, in our
trench, bombarded as it continually was, a
little house cat prowling about and asking for
caresses.

On the Saturday night we were told that
we might have to retire from the position
that had cost so much to win and to hold,
owing to the success of the German attack
on our left. It would have been a pretty

K

risky manœuvre. We made all arrangements for bluffing the enemy. Morning broke, and with it the glad news that the Hill was to be held.

From my own experience I can testify to the accuracy of the German artillery, and those here in hospital who took part in the counter-attack say their musketry is good. They certainly had plenty of ammunition.

It is said that the Germans have been making frequent use of explosive bullets. What really happens is that the soldiers themselves sometimes take out the bullet from the cartridge and reverse it, with the blunt end forward. It makes no great difference to the accuracy of a shot at close range, but makes a terrible wound. Again, 'explosive' wounds may be caused by ricochets, and this is a still more likely explanation.

May 1st.

The King and Queen paid us a surprise visit today. They each spoke to us all individually; first the Queen went down the ward and then the King. I had no idea that they were in the building till the Queen appeared in my cubicle.

The King asked me where I was wounded, and in what fight, and how long I had been in the regiment, and other questions. He asked me what was my regiment, and when I told him he remarked, 'Oh, yes, my regiment'. Then in his capacity as Colonel-in-Chief, he told me off for having such a dirty kilt (it was hanging on the wall, the tartan quite obliterated in mud), which little joke seemed to please him much. Very nice of them to come and cheer us up. Though we are all thankful to be here!

[Follows a period of leave, and a holiday at Arundel. Then about a month at the 3rd Battalion training camp on the Cromarty Firth, a very happy time, with Arthur, and other friends. There were visits to Inverness and Strathpeffer, and particularly a day spent on board the 'King George V'.

The ward-room was very interested in getting first-hand information from the trenches, as they had little idea of the state of things, cut off as they are. They kept up a fire of questions, which I did my best to answer, though I was glad when they responded by showing me all over the battleship. Most interesting for me. The Duke of Leeds was an intelligence officer on board, and he asked me a number of questions about life in Flanders.

The Northern air and the hills were a real tonic; I never spent a happier month. I made but one entry in my diary during this period.]

July 23rd.

Today finds me in camp all day, as it is my turn to act as orderly officer or subaltern of the day, and to trot about kilted, gaitered, and girt with a (borrowed) basket-hilted sword. One's day begins early, for it is necessary to rise at 3.30, so as to turn out and inspect the guard before 4; and up to 11 o'clock at night one runs around and inspects food stores and quarters, changes the guards, visits the hospital, smells the meat, and does all manner of jobs, including the hearing of complaints, if any. I am quite enjoying myself, because I can see how the routine work of this great camp is carried on. Everything is wonderfully organized, and the men have every comfort possible, with good food, well cooked.

A fellow home from the first battalion told
me that one night an officer gave orders that
two very dead cows near the trenches they
had taken over were to be buried, as the
stench was abominable. Every man of the
party sent was sick, the cows were so far gone.
He made two attempts himself to get near
them, and was himself sick each time. He
then sent a message to Brigade Head-quarters
asking what he should do. The officer there,
indignant at being awakened out of sleep by
such a message, replied that he had better
write to Sir John French for a hyena to eat
them up!

[Early in August I left for France again,
and stayed for six weeks in Rouen base camp,
La Bruyère, among the heather and the
pines. We did not have much work to do,
and I had some fine walks and trips on the
river to La Boulie, and other places. Also,
I did a lot of sketching, making great friends
with a wounded Frenchman named Raymond
Desvarreux. He is a well-known battle
painter (*hors concours*) and was executing a
French Government commission to paint
studies of British types at Rouen. He gave

me much help, and we studied the fine collection in Rouen together.

The weather all the time was glorious; but all good things come to an end, and a day or two after the great attack at Loos I had orders to go up the line once more, to the 1st Battalion this time.

September 29th.

Arrived here last night—I am a little uncertain how to spell the name of the village —and hope to leave today. We hear distant booms now and again, just to remind us there is a war on, and the rain pours down incessantly in the good old way.

I left Rouen yesterday with a draft for a Territorial battalion in our division. I was fortunate in being in the same coach as the Train Conducting Officer, and his servant brought us tea from his kitchen, and water, so I had a wash, a shave, and not being uncomfortably crowded, a good sleep also.

We detrained at Choques (I think it's called) and tramped from thence up to this depressing dorp which I believe is named Mazingarbe. I found a billet for my men, or rather some rough shelter only, for a cartshed was the best I could do. They were very tired and hungry, and I tried to buy them some food, but I had very little cash with me, and among 80 men a few loaves — not many were to be had — did not go far.

At Divisional H.Q. here nobody with red tabs on seemed to have any idea where the regiment was. I was furious at this; if this is a sample of staff work no wonder we are taking our time winning the war. They didn't know and seemed to care less, but at length I found a weary overworked subaltern who told me it was still in the line. However, the Town Major turned out to be one of 'ours', happily, so it was fortunate I thought of applying to him. He gave me a helping hand. He was living comfortably in what was once a monastery, and I had a regular Scots tea with him.

Discovered a brother officer in a billet at the Mairie. He was just off to join the battalion, so I slept—O luxury!—in his room in a bed with sheets. I cannot of course leave my unfortunate draft until I can hand them over to someone who will look after them. No one seems to know where their unit is,

However, I obtained rations for them, so they are tolerably happy.

The village is crammed with troops. There is a big show going on, but I don't know at all what is happening. The air quivers with gunfire, and the sky is alight at night.

September 30th.

Found a home for my Territorials.

October 1st.

Noeux-les-Mines. This is a filthy little mining village, slippery with black mud, and overshadowed by huge slag heaps. Having had to march up from rail-head with that draft, my valise, containing all I possess, has gone adrift somewhere in this miserable country. I only found Divisional H.Q. by a happy chance at Mazingarbe, miles away from where I was told it would be, and there, as I said, no one knew the whereabouts of the battalion H.Q. staff; so no wonder the lorry driver, to whom I entrusted it, went astray. Most inconvenient.

The Brigade was relieved from the German trenches they had taken, the night I arrived. It was a shocking sight to see the battalion march into billets when morning came. Pale and weary, plastered from head to foot with white chalk and mud, what was left of them stepped out desperately to the pipers playing. Only two officers who went over the top remain. I am commanding the, remnant of D Company.

Very busy reorganizing.

The country round here is typical of the territory the British Army fights in; flat, with incredible quantities of mud.

Hope we shall move to more comfortable quarters before going up the line again, for the men's sake, as they are so muddy, after the rain in the trenches. They really need a long rest. I had to be quite ruthless with the wretched civilians to get a roof over my men at all.

The Boche seems to have taken a bit of a knock, anyhow.

October 2nd.

Making up my kit from dead officers' stock. Weather is a little better, and drafts of new officers and men are beginning to arrive. Flies are a great nuisance here, everything is black with them.

Very busy getting the company cleaned up and re-equipped.

October 3rd.

The Jocks' French is sometimes very funny. The expression 'n'a plus' (short for 'il n'y a plus'), used by the little shopkeepers to mean they are out of stock of some article, is rendered in the soldiers' letters (which I have to censor) as 'na-poo' or 'napu'. Then 'Bonswong' is rather a curious way of spelling 'Bon soir'.

Every morning at Réveillé the pipers march up and down the street in front of our billets playing, and also outside the tiny fly-blown place where our battalion mess is, just as they do at home.

What a medley of noise is going on outside! Booming motor-cars, racketing lorries, throbbing motor-cycles, rattle of hoofs on the *pavé*, roar of wheels and jingle of harness, the tramp of marching men, talk and song and shout, shrill screeches from the railway station, motor horns, thud-thud of anti-aircraft guns, and through all the incessant whop-thump of 'Mother' and 'Grandmother' a few kilometres away.

We are more or less refitted and re-equipped by now, though the bulk of the company consists of drafts, all fresh from home, and not really fit for the trying time ahead of us. The great difficulty is the lack of experienced N.C.O.'s and junior officers.

Later. Soon came the order to make ready to go up the line again. It was pouring with rain, and when we were all dressed in our trench kit, and hung round with revolver, ammunition, map case, haversack, water-bottle, pack, and other trimmings, we company commanders were instructed to proceed in advance, mounted, as far as possible, to take over from the unit we were relieving.

Riding with all that impedimenta, in the rain, and *in a kilt*, bare skin to the saddle, like an ancient Greek, was no joke, but we trotted away along the *pavé*. My kilt and waterproof 'rode' up, and my hose came down, so I exposed bare legs from thigh to ankle, which would have been amusing had there been anyone about to laugh.

Eventually we reached a battered heap of bricks that had been the hamlet of Philosophe. The spot was a desert; rubble and chalk and

broken bricks, disembowelled mules, bully-
beef tins, rusty muddy rifles, rounds of
ammunition, discarded equipment, unex-
ploded shells, shell-holes filled with yellow
water, stench, and silence. Here we dis-
mounted under cover of a fold in the ground.
C. and I swung off our horses, forgetting the
weight on our backs, slipped on the mud,
and sat down hard, to the mild astonishment
of our horses, who turned their Roman noses
round at us. Laughing, we picked ourselves
up, and from this point guides led us through
the gathering dusk to our positions, where we
took over from the company commanders of
the Norfolks. Here I met a friend who was
serving in the ranks of the Norfolks, and had
a long talk with him while awaiting the
arrival of my men.

Followed a trying tour in the trenches with
untried soldiers, with inexperienced subalterns
and N.C.O.'s. It meant almost sleeplessness
for me. Two young officers from Sandhurst
joined the company, good fellows, but natur-
ally new to the life. But they soon settled
down.

All this time I was snowed under with
detailed staff orders for an attack by the

battalion, which I personally thought almost bound to fail under the conditions laid down. I frankly told the C.O. so. 'I can't help it, my boy,' said he, 'they are divisional orders.' The details might have been left to the colonel, or at any rate the brigadier, instead of being drawn up by staff wallahs away behind, who did not seem to grasp the situation at all. I admire the C.O. very much, he is the best type of Scottish gentleman, and a good soldier too.

October 13th.

The attack is over: an utter failure. We were opposite a few mounds of rubble still known as the village of Hulluch, close to the famous Hohenzollern Redoubt.

There were two sand-bag barricades at the end of my trench. There were about 20 yards of No-Man's Land between the two barricades, and the trench beyond the second one was occupied by the enemy. D Company's job was to break down our barricade, rush with bombs the German one, scale it with ladders, and drive the enemy along, while the other companies attacked over the top.

Our artillery was well-ranged and fire was continuous for hours, but little real damage was done, as the enemy was in deep dug-outs, such as those captured a fortnight before. Still, there was an exciting whirlwind of shells, noise, and smoke, shells skimming over our heads with a scream and a whistle, crashing blackly on to the chalk parapets over the way. Just before zero hour our fellows put some gas over, but the wind shifted and I think the gas only added to the confusion. All this gas and bombardment gave the enemy the plainest possible idea of what to expect, and, in my opinion, our only chance would have been a surprise raid, preferably at night.

I was definitely ordered by the C.O. to remain at company head-quarters (a little scoop out of the side of the trench) to receive reports, so I had to put one of my subalterns, MacD., in charge of the bombing party. Though outwardly cheerful I felt sick when I told him. He looked grave, and stared far away over my head. Then he said 'All right' quietly and resolutely, and went back to his men. I felt I loved him.

At last zero hour came, the bombardment

lifted, and I knew that MacD. must have gone over the ruins of our barricade. I stayed back at my 'head-quarters' tortured with anxiety. The arrangement was he would send along a message as soon as he was in the German trench.

But nothing seemed to be happening and no word came. I guessed things had miscarried, and I pushed my way along the trench. Presently I met the bayonet men who were supposed to follow the bombers, edging back. They were mostly recruits, and were leaderless and much shaken. They cried out that the officer was killed by the barricade. Waving my revolver I scrambled past them, cursing them vigorously, but I could no more have hurt the dear lads than I could have shot my mother. I reached the spot where our barricade had been, caught one terrible glimpse of a heap of bodies, and, I remember, someone's hand cut neatly off at the wrist and grasping a bomb like a cricket ball, when a bomb shaped like a hairbrush came over the German barricade, and fell hissing at my feet. I swung round on my heel, and it exploded behind me, blowing me off my feet.

The shock was so severe that I really thought I was done for, and lay still for a few moments, but very soon I realized the spot was so unhealthy from falling bombs that I had better get out of it. I found I could crawl, and managed to get back to where our barricade had been, or rather a few yards behind that spot. There I thought I would try and stand up. I succeeded in doing so, and began to feel I wasn't so badly hurt after all. There was a group of grey-faced men some distance down the trench staring at me. I exhorted and implored them to come forward and rebuild the barricade, as it was obvious some defence had to be made. Our little show had failed, and for all I knew there might be a bombing counter-attack any minute. No one moved for a little while, they were all too shaken, but presently one of the survivors of the bombing party shouted, 'I'm wi' ye, lad,' and ran to me. We started to haul sand-bags into position, and then others trickled forward and they set to with a will. This stout fellow had no rifle, so I gave him my revolver.[1] I was feeling faint by this time, with my kilt in ribbons and my

[1] Which he kept for me for a year, until he was killed.

backside in a bloody mess, and a dull sick pain inside, so leaving him in charge temporarily, I went to find the other subaltern.

I found him sick and shaken by his first action, and sitting as though paralysed, but I roused him, and left him in charge of the job (where I hear he did well) while I sought the M.O. to get the wound dressed. The Germans were shelling us now, and spurts of bullets broke and cracked all along the parapets. I saw one rip through the water-jacket of our Vickers gun as I limped along.

The M.O. seemed to think I could not be patched up in the trench, so he sent me down to the Casualty Clearing Station, in charge of two stretcher-bearers. The trenches were too narrow for a stretcher so I had to walk somehow. There was a lot of shelling, and the stretcher-bearers were risking their lives, and when we came to the open, I told them to go back and leave me. They refused, but eventually, as it seemed impossible to reach Lone Tree where the C.C.S. was, they assisted me down the steps of a deep dug-out and laid me down with the other wounded. They were fine fellows and did not care a damn for the shells; their only thought was

L

for me. I would not let them come any farther, and had no desire whatever to go on myself!

I must have lost consciousness for many hours, for when I came-to the dug-out was dark and deserted. All the other wounded had gone, and possibly I had been left for dead. Anyway, I tried to call out, and at length attracted the attention of some men outside, who came down, helped me up, and over the open in the dark to the C.C.S. at Lone Tree. I vaguely remember the doctor recognizing me as an old schoolfellow, being put in a train, and into an ambulance car, in which the jolting was agonizing.

October 17th.

The car unloaded me at the Duchess of Westminster's Hospital at Le Touquet, a spacious, beautiful place. The first thing I remember is a number of red-tabbed doctors round my bed, asking questions.

Later (undated).

I stayed here some time, and received the greatest kindness from everyone, from the Duchess herself to the ward orderly. I was on the danger list for a fortnight, for I had some tiny fragments of bomb-casing in the intestines somewhere, but everything healed up all right. My mother and father came over and stayed at the hotel till I was off the list.

Then followed evacuation to England, and a short period in hospital at Myatt's Park, Camberwell, and a week or two's holiday at Torquay with H. M., who was wounded and convalescing in the same hospital.

1916

1916

January 5th.

MARRIED Norah, a glad day.

January 6th–20th.

Honeymoon at Bath. Can't write in this book.

March and April (various entries undated).

Most of the time snow has lain on the ground. Have been on 'light duty' at Sutton Veney on Salisbury Plain, near Warminster.

This 'light duty' turned out to be exceedingly hard work. The division (a T.F. one) was training for the front, and I was attached to a battalion as a platoon officer, having to work as hard as anyone during their intensive training.

The Plain is glorious, and though I found things rather tiring, it was interesting enough, and I had some riding in Longleat Park. Norah and I managed to secure lodgings in Warminster, though I didn't see much of her, unfortunately. They kept my nose down to it so.

I had applied for a permanent Regular commission in the regiment, and while I was here I was gazetted afresh, starting, in spite of my protest, from the bottom again as the junior second-lieutenant. So now I take orders from boys who a week ago were buying their Sam Browne belts.

At the end of April I was posted once more to the training battalion. The day after I arrived I went out riding, and turning too sharply out of a gate, I hurt my left knee against the iron post and was lamed by synovitis in consequence. I was useless for work, so got a few days' leave, and stayed with H. M. up at Glen Urquhart, where we trolled for salmon on Loch Ness. This was my second visit to his place, having had a day's shooting there last year with his brother.

From there I went to the Scottish Command Bombing School at Troon, on the Ayrshire coast, where we had one fortnight of very strenuous work. We lived well in the big

hotel, and in the week-end I had some riding
on the sands.

On Easter Sunday two or three of us waded
out to a wreck at low tide, and it being sunny,
stripped and dropped into the sea for one
brief ice-cold minute, emerging with a gasping
yell, and drying ourselves with pocket hand-
kerchiefs.

Found a baby seal on the rocks.

Each morning Goat Fell in Arran loomed
across the Firth, and Ailsa Craig stood out
sharply or faded into haze.

Then next week to Glasgow *en route* for
the North. I stayed the night at Perth, in-
tending to pick up the train from London at
dawn (Norah was on it), but a Zeppelin
wandered by that night scattering bombs,
which delayed things. However, the train
at length arrived, and we had breakfast together at Kingussie.

Then we spent a happy week with some
delightful people on a farm a few miles from
camp. We had a day on board the battleship 'Marlborough' as the guests of the
surgeon-commander. It was fine to see from
the leaping picket-boat the long lines of grey
hulls of the Battle Fleet in the roadstead,

against the snow-capped hills of the Ben Wyvis range, and a dark stormy sky.

I was given the job of raising and training a band of scouts and snipers from the battalion, which was paraded for me so that I could pick my own men. It was too good a life to last; after a week I was ordered to France.

May 11th.

My twenty-sixth birthday: I left England via Southampton–Havre by the ordinary packet.

Had a bath at Rouen, encountering the (to me) unusual but doubtless sanitary custom of draping the bath with clean sheets; and went up the line almost at once to the 1st Battalion in the mining country round Calonne and Les Brébis, a wilderness of chalky poppy-grown trenches running in a maze through or over slag-heaps, ruined villages, smashed pit-heads, and abandoned coal trucks. Many of our trenches were actually on the warm, smoking slag-heaps. They have been alight since before the war! Some of the communication trenches have been revetted by their former occupants, the French, with pitprops. One is called Birdcage Walk. This is all very well until a shell comes, when the fallen props make it impassable.

My arrival at Calonne coincided with a gas-shell bombardment of the village, and for hours that sunny afternoon I sat in a house unable to eat, smoke, sleep, or read, but could only cough and wipe my eyes.

May 16th.

It is curious how so often in this war one sees little of one's enemy. I have seen remarkably few Germans. Today, however, I had an interesting peep at the Boche. We had a sniper's observation post rigged up underneath a railway truck, cunningly hidden, and from it we could see away behind the German lines, and watch through telescopes their men strolling about in the open. I had seen so little of the enemy for so long that I got the same sort of thrill that one gets deer-stalking when a deer is sighted out of range.

May 17th.

The trench life is fairly quiet, no attacks or raids on our battalion sector, but we have no heavy artillery—nothing bigger than a few 4·5 howitzers—it has all gone somewhere; so the German trench-mortars and five-nines make life exciting, and cause a constant trickle of casualties. A still sunny afternoon, not a sound to be heard anywhere, the men asleep, curled up on the fire-step. A sudden tearing crescendo whistle, a bump and a tremor, cries and groans from along the trench. These five-nines put the fear of God into me.

My nerves are under control, and I can do my job all right, but I am feeling the strain in a way I used not to do. I often find my-self speaking sharply when there is no need for it. The men, too, seem different; they no longer want 'Jerry' to come over, as they used to declare in the old days. But all seem confident that the Big Push will end trench warfare this year.

There are several deep dug-outs in this sector, underground caverns reached by steps, on the German plan. They save lives in a bombardment, but are bad for morale; it is terribly hard to drag oneself out once you are safely in! However, the balance is in favour of them, because bombardment in an open trench is not exactly good for the nerves.

May 18*th*.

Last night some enemy activity was expected, and the company officer detailed a N.C.O. and a party of men to occupy a deserted stretch of trench on our right flank. Unfortunately the Germans selected this bit for a trench-mortar bombardment. I happened to be in a dug-out near, and heard and felt a tremendous concussion. I clambered up the steps and out into the trench, and looking up saw a shower of sparks like a falling rocket, followed by another great detonation. They were evidently ranging on the newly-manned sector. It was too much for the luckless party there, who came streaming back, white-faced and shaking with terror. To enable them to recover their tone I made them stand on the steps of the dug-out ready to come out at a moment's notice to repel any attack. None came, but if they had stayed where they were they would have been in no fit state to deal with it, so the dug-out had its uses.

Our reply to these trench mortars is the Stokes mortar, not such a big shell, but far more rapid and accurate. They are now

beginning to arrive here, and it is said they
are putting the wind up the Germans.

I am sorry for the Stokes gun officers.
They have a nerve-racking job, and nobody loves them, because their activities draw
fire.

May 24th.

Wiring is a rotten job, and everyone is glad
to come in when it is over. You get out of
the trench, preferably on a dark night, and
wander off some yards in front with a party
loaded up with stakes and coils of barbed
wire. The stakes have to be driven in as
noiselessly as possible; sometimes we have a
sort of trestle shaped like a knife-rest, and
wire is festooned and tangled up on the wood.
In the early days one fancied that when the
Verey lights went up one *must* be seen, but
in fact the bright light has a very restricted
area of illumination, and if you stay still you
will most likely be unobserved.

Talking of Verey lights, tonight I went by
myself to a deserted trench which ran out
towards the enemy, just to reconnoitre and
see whether it need be manned. One of these
rockets suddenly landed almost at my feet,

fizzled flaring on the ground, and leapt at
me. I turned and fled down the sap with
this thing fizzing and bouncing at my heels,
till it at length expired, and I stopped in
utter darkness, cursing myself for getting
windy at nothing.

May 26th.

A typical day in these trenches begins at
dawn, with 'Stand to'. The N.C.O.'s jerk
the men out of their heavy sleep—the private
soldier seems to have the power of dropping
off into deep slumber in the most uncomfortable positions—and plant them on the fire-step,
where they yawn and rub their eyes, and
begin to clean their rifles, before the inspecting officer comes round. One or two
men in every fire-bay has been by turns on
sentry duty all night. I make the round of
my platoon accompanied by my platoon
sergeant, inspecting rifles, bombs, and gas-
masks.

This duty over, 'Stand down' is given, day
sentries are posted, and I go off to my dug-
out for a shave, provided things are quiet.
The men prepare their breakfast, and we
officers have ours, and settle down for the

day's routine. This may be quite peaceful, or we may be harassed by trench mortars or some five-nines.

If so annoyed, there is no rest for anyone, and it is no use ringing up the artillery for retaliation, for we seem to have nothing heavier behind us than divisional four-fives, which seem unable to knock out the trench-mortar emplacement. I have spotted exactly where it is, and have tried the divisional artillery on it, but their ammunition seems rationed, and nothing they can do seems any good. It is said that the heavy stuff has left us for an 'unknown' destination. Everywhere are rumours of the Big Push. Today I was on company duty till 2 o'clock, snatching a bite of lunch, nevertheless. Then a blessed rest till tea at 5, though personally I can seldom sleep in the front line.

At dusk we all 'stood to' again, and got ready for the night's work. One of us is in charge of a wiring party, another of a trench-repairing gang, while a third—my turn to-night—will go round the company front, inspect all posts and sentries, and be generally responsible. And it is going to rain!

So it goes on, day after day, and night after

night, when we get our rations and evacuate our casualties, if any.

June 6th.

Relief is well named. It is indeed a relief to go back to billets. Physically we are tired out at the end of the tour, and for those with any responsibility the mental relief is great too.

The day the news of Jutland came through was a Sunday, and we were at Church Parade in Les Brébis. I was standing opposite to Andrew, and the thought passed through my mind, as my eye caught his M.C. ribbon, that I wished I could collect one.

My astonishment was great when, after the National Anthem, the Colonel, who was standing beside me, turned to me and said, 'I hear you have the Military Cross. Is it true?' I hadn't the faintest idea, but newspapers were being sold in the town that day, and there it was in the King's Birthday List in the 'Daily Telegraph'.

Here in Les Brébis during our rest period I made friends with a gunner officer in charge of a six-inch gun. He was a musician, and had a piano in his billet, and used to play

M

Grieg to us in the evenings. We had some rat-hunts, too, with terriers; sticks, and half-bricks.

Talking of rat-hunts, there were some rats as big as cats in our trench (or seemed so by moonlight), and we started potting at them with our revolvers. When they saw the flashes, the Germans actually fired some whizz-bangs at us, and made us run.

The other day, lying underneath a truck, I watched the enemy artillery trying to knock down a pit-head chimney stack. No doubt they thought we might use it as an observation post, though I do not know how we could get up there. They hit it fair and square in the end, and it crashed in a smother of red dust.

June 18*th.*

A day or two ago we had the excitement of seeing a German kite-balloon destroyed. We heard the faint hum of an aeroplane, and suddenly where the gas-bag floated was just a cloud of white smoke.

The C.O. has made me Scout and Sniping Officer, with a gang of men to train. This is a job I thoroughly enjoy, though the material I had to deal with is most town-bred Clyde-siders. We have been some time in the trenches round Calonne, and have got them into first-rate order. And they are spotlessly tidy, not a scrap of rubbish anywhere showing. I don't think the Guards would show a better line in the same circumstances.

June 20th.

My platoon has been relieved. We emerged safely out of the communication trench, and steadily slouched (you cannot call it marched) through a deserted ruined village back to billets. The going was pretty good, for we were no longer loaded up with bags of bombs and sand-bags full of rations as on the outward journey, and was not a hot drink and a good sleep ahead of us? We were very muddy, and very dirty, and very weary from lack of sleep during the last few days and nights, but were in good spirits. Soon we abandoned single file and closed up into fours. The leading four padded along, whistling and singing, God bless them:

> 'He's a man of wonderful audacity,
> Private Michael Cassidy,
> V.C.!'

July 1st.

Gunfire to the south has been growing greater and greater, and today, so we hear from Brigade Signals Office, the British Army went over the top on the Somme front.

July 10th.

A week ago our division had orders to go south and reinforce, and we were pulled out of the line. We had a short train journey, and marched for three days the rest of the way.

It did us good to stretch our legs, and though the unaccustomed marching was trying after trench warfare, I think we all enjoyed it. I marched at the head of the battalion with my scouts and snipers (pronounced scoots and sneepers), and one day had the honour (so I felt it to be, the greatest in my life) of being at the head of this famous division of the B.E.F. on the march on active service; my own little command stepping out behind me, then the pipers and drummers, then the Colonel on his horse, and the miles of marching men.

This back area of the Somme in its summer green is unspoilt and undulating, and is a sight for sore eyes after the muck-heaps of the Nord. We have no illusions about the dirty work ahead of us, but we try to think as little about that as possible. A soldier must live in the present, for his past is dead, and his future—the prospect of death.

July 11*th.*

This evening we reached Albert, a town frequently shelled, but still recognizable as a town, with the golden Madonna and Child hanging head down from the tall red tower. The spot is a lively one, as, in spite of the advance of July 1st, it is still within heavy artillery range. We stayed the night here.

July 12*th.*

This morning we made for Bécourt Wood. In a sand-bag shelter in the wood I found two novels—'Exton Manor' by Archibald Marshall, and 'Justice' by Galsworthy, which I have annexed.

A first impression of the Somme front is an immense rolling green-brown expanse of bare upland pitted and seamed in all directions with white chalk trenches, scarred here and there with heaps of rubble, blotched with woods consisting of trees snapped and splintered; swarms of men, horses, and guns everywhere; the boom and crash of artillery, and to emphasize the atmosphere of menace, aeroplanes glinting in the sun and humming far overhead, surrounded by little white puffs of smoke, and here and there an observation balloon hanging in the sky.

Round Fricourt, which was taken on the 1st, the country is being tidied up. Much of the village is simply red powder, and the ruined houses, still standing in fragments, are being pulled down for road material, for new roads are being made everywhere. Soon there will be nothing left but the large black-and-white notice-board.

All about are huge shell-holes, dead bodies from both sides, the dreadful battle-field litter of rifles, bombs, shells, steel helmets, equipment, and letters, German letters from home chiefly. The dead are being buried as fast as possible, sometimes being dug out for identification and re-interred, and equipment salved.

The deep German dug-outs are marvellous, real underground galleries and rooms. How our men took this line I don't know.

The battalion played a passive part in our first scrap on the Somme, the taking of a village called Contalmaison. We were in an old German support trench while some other crowd did the attack, which was successful. We endured a good deal of shelling, which was a rather nervy business, but it did little damage.

I was talking to the second in command most of the time, watching the shells plunge into the ground just in front of us as we leant against the parapet, but trying to pretend we didn't mind. Later on I went along a few yards to have a look round when a field-gun shell seemed to explode right at my feet. I was just touched by a splinter, but was quite unhurt. A man close by had his shirt and coat torn off. His bare back was quite covered with blood. He was crying with fright, while waiting his turn with the doctor, but I think he was only very slightly hurt.

When all was quiet not long afterwards I went up to Contalmaison. It had changed hands several times, and the mile or so of grassland between was heaped with English and German dead who had fallen in attack and counter-attack. One huge German had evidently been blown up by a shell. He lay all doubled up, his bones broken and protruding. The wind carried the heavy smell of death and corruption over the grass.

Contalmaison itself consisted of about half a wall of a church, some dug-outs, rusty wire, an obscene green scummy pool, a few dead horses, and a smell. The garrison was underground somewhere, and not visible.

July 14*th.*

The second great defensive lines were taken on this day. We again had no hand in it. The dug-outs underground were even more surprising than before, of great length and depth, but our heavy shells had blown in one or two nevertheless. The rest of the trenches were ruinous. One dug-out I saw had probably been used as a casualty clearing station, there being an ingenious shute down which one could lower stretchers. Another was big enough to hold a company deep underground, with a private room and a bed and a table for the officer, with a picture of the Kaiser, and a glazed door.

July 16th.

Today I had to go up to a post the other side of Mametz Wood. I walked through the wood—a ghastly, gruesome place, silent, but made more jumpy by the echoing crash of an occasional shell. It was littered with British and German dead, faces blackened with H.E., and half hidden by the undergrowth or lying in the muddy rides, which were pitted with shell-holes filled with water; and odds and ends of rubbish all over the place, and splintered trees. I saw a whole row of our men lying at the edge of the wood just as if they were alive, their rifles gripped in their hands. Another thing that I noticed was a very good-looking tall German boy who had pitched on his back, and lay there peacefully with his steel helmet on, his lips parted showing good white teeth, a well-bred lad, a volunteer, I expect.

My life was saved today by my steel helmet. I was standing talking to one or two others when a 5·9 burst some little way off. We did not take much notice of it, but some seconds later there was a 'ding', and a jagged piece of iron that had evidently shot high into the air came down and made a dent on the very crown of my steel hat. It would have made more than a dent in my skull. Pity we didn't have the helmets earlier. How many would have been saved in the trench warfare!

July 20th.

Today near Bazentin we watched an attack launched about a mile away on our left. It was a terrible incident of modern war. There was suddenly a noise like the mad beating of hundreds of mighty drums, and every second or two a great crash; a rolling cloud of dust and smoke arose from the plain, and moved slowly forward, the whole inferno dying as suddenly as it began. From first to last we could distinguish no living creature, and what happened we never knew.

A 'dog fight'. The westering sun is throwing a rosy glow on the eastern sky. Low down, away behind the enemy trenches, the rose is dotted and smeared with little tufts of black shrapnel. Among these ever-appearing dots and smears tiny specks are moving, twisting, and wheeling. Now and again one sinks in a vertical stream of smoke. Men come out of dug-outs and shelters, and stand in the trench, gazing fascinated. Presently the fight is broken off, and soon there comes the engine song of the returning squadron, as it drones home overhead to rest, and to tell the tale of those left behind and of foes put down.

July 24th.

Another mess-up; any number of good men lost and nothing to show for it.

We were supposed to attack opposite Martinpuich, near High Wood; but our heavy artillery preparation went all wrong for a start, as most of the big stuff plumped into our own trenches. It was sickening to watch this helplessly from battalion H.Q., while we made desperate efforts to get the information back to the scattered batteries.

I suddenly spied two panic-stricken Jocks blundering back from the trenches over the open. I went out and brought them in to the C.O. I don't suppose the case will go further, partly because the C.O. is human and understanding, and partly for the honour of the regiment. I think he let them recover themselves and sent them back.

I am sure my life was saved by the C.O.
telling me to stay with him at head-quarters.
He wanted me to go up to the front afterwards and report on the situation, which I did
—rather a gloomy state of 'as-you-were',
with many good officers and men lost.

The Australians are great lads. 'Where's
this Pozieres? Where's this blasted village
nobody can take? We want it!' And they
had it.

The men nearly all smoke cigarettes now,
very few smoke pipes, with the result that
the tobacco ration is largely wasted, and there
is always a shortage of cigarettes. I bought
some cigarette-papers at the E.F. Canteen
the other day, and am trying to get the men
to use them with the tobacco.

August 8th.

We are having a peaceful happy rest away
behind Albert, at Baisieux, in lovely unspoilt
country, cornfields, woods, leafy trees, and
streams. The officers are quartered in an
orchard on a farm under canvas shelters,
shaded from the glaring sun. The swallows
wheel and twitter in the blue sky.

During this brief period of rest I can add

to this record various little things that have escaped notice before.

The C.O. and some others. I have never really thought about whether the C.O. is popular or not (I am sure he doesn't care), I should say he probably is, but all I know is that I like him greatly. He is quiet and reserved in manner, never utters a hasty word, but is a good disciplinarian in his quiet way. His hair is greying, and so is his moustache, his face is lined a little, and puckered at the eyes; the eyes are kind, responsibility is leaving its mark on him, but he is always steady, cool, and self-possessed. I don't know where or how he won his D.S.O., but I know it was deserved.

Cuming-Seton is one who may do well in the regiment if he lives. We have always been friends since we shared a hut for six weeks at Rouen, though I suppose we have not much in common really. He is an O.E. Some people did not like his rather too cock-sure manner when he joined up first from Cambridge, but I personally look below that, there is good metal underneath.

McBride, who has been doing Adjutant for some time, is, I believe, an Edinburgh lawyer in civil life, an older man than most of us, keen and competent.

B.-B. is one of the best of the bunch. A Regular, probably from one of the Scottish public schools, handsome and brave.

MacBrae is a Tyne-sider, an ex-quarter-master sergeant who has served in India, and like most rankers, but not all, not too well liked by the men. He is apt to be fussy and bullying in matters of detail. Probably a case of a good N.C.O. spoilt by a commission and too much whisky.

MacRimmon is an Edinburgh lawyer, but young, rather a nice fellow. He and Mac-Brae, an ill-assorted couple, went to Amiens together one day. MacRimmon spent his time with one of the frolic ladies of that city, while MacBrae had too much to drink. Each thought the other rather disgusting.

As regards the doctor, he is a white man if ever there was one, and where the five-nines fall thickest, there he is.

As for the men, the pity is that one gets so little opportunity of knowing them. The Jocks do not wear their hearts on their sleeves, and it takes a good while to get inside their minds, and life is so short. Almost before you have learnt their names some change is made, or you lose half of them in action.

I am getting to know and to like my scouts and snipers, though.

I never knew a bit what my old platoon thought of me, but they paid me the compliment of saying they wished they had me with them in the Martinpuich show. My feelings are rather mixed.

Decorations. I do not pretend that I am not pleased at having a bit of ribbon to wear. Before coming to the Somme the general pinned the ribbon on my breast and shook hands. Of course it doesn't cut much ice here; too many good deeds go unrecognized for that, but one's wife and parents will be glad. And after all, my Military Cross 'came up with the rations' as the saying is; probably the battalion had one allotted, and they had to give it to someone. The only excuse I can think of for it is the Hulluch show, and Lord knows I did little enough there except get wounded.

Soft jobs. Had the chance of a home appointment when I was at Troon before I came out. Turned it down; must see the show through while perfectly fit. There is too much dodging going on. This may sound priggish: but that's what I think. Besides, I really like being with the men, and I'm proud of being in the regiment.

P.H. helmets. There is only one thing worse than a prolonged wearing of a gas-mask, and that is being gassed. The P.H. helmet is an impregnated bag of grey flannel, which is placed over the head, the ends of which are placed under the jacket, which is buttoned over it round the neck. There are eye-pieces, and you breathe through a rubber valve or nozzle, which you hold in your teeth. We have to inspect the men's masks frequently; as usual they are hopelessly casual; the other day in the front line I found an eye-piece missing from one in my platoon. This meant certain death if gas came over.

August 10th.

I am getting my scouts fit and active again. Three days ago I found a number of them green in the face, very sick, suffering severely from excessive indulgence in some villainous white wine, or 'vinnblank' as they love to call it. I read them a severe lecture, telling them to stick to beer, and keep off this poisonous wine, and when they had recovered, I took the two worst offenders out with me on a tour of exploration to find a suitable bathing-place within an easy route march for the battalion. We covered about 20 miles of country, and I brought them back well lathered and dog-weary. But they stuck it gamely. They well knew I was teaching them the lesson that scouts have got to keep fit.

We found a bathing-place after much difficulty, an idyllic spot like a painting by Alfred East, a long, flowery meadow surrounded by tall trees, where the battalion could sit at ease, an approach for the field-cookers, and a stream flowing through just deep enough to swim in.

I guided the battalion there a few days later, and we had a most enjoyable day. There was a row about it afterwards, because the Town Major complained on behalf of the inhabitants (it was just outside a village) and the C.O. wanted to know why I had omitted to ask for permission. I told him that such places were very hard to find, and if I had asked for permission, I should probably have been refused, and there would

N

have been no bathing. He said it seemed a very good reason, but suggested that the bathing should not be repeated.

Often in this glorious weather B.-B., the doctor, and I have long canters over the bare uplands, our long shadows with us in the slanting rays of the evening sun, and a golden haze of dust around us as we ride.

We saw a fine battalion of French troops pass through today. Young, strong, healthy, sun-burnt men they were, well equipped and in good spirits. They marched at a good pace, but just go-as-you-please; march discipline as we know it seems unknown in the French Army. Later we learnt it was the famous Iron Division, from Verdun.

August 13th.

During June, before leaving the mining area, a notice had come round asking young officers to volunteer for the R.F.C. in view of the great contemplated expansion of this branch; and I was so sick of trenches (and trench mortars) that I had sent in my name, on the principle of anything for a change. After all, it only meant being seconded for a while, we did not have to leave the regiment.

Today an order suddenly came for me and another subaltern to report for examination by a Royal Flying Corps selecting officer at rail-head (Méricourt).

We went. The examination took this form:

Q. Have you any engineering experience?

A. No, sir.

Q. Can you drive a car?

A. No, sir.

Q. And you think you can be a pilot?

A. Yes, sir.

Q. Can you ride or sail a boat?

A. I can ride.

Q. What games do you play?

A. Rugger; I was in my School XV and have played a lot since; cricket and tennis, of course.

Q. And you seriously consider that you can tackle a pilot's job?

A. Certainly, sir.

Q. Right! Here's your ticket to London town, and good luck to you. The train leaves this evening.

We came out into the dust and sunshine, and listened to the guns throbbing in the distance. 'The train leaves this evening'! England!! Norah!!!

November 14*th*.

The last two months have gone swiftly. I am now a pilot seconded to the Royal Flying Corps. After a few days' leave in August, which Norah and I spent at Rye, I reported to Shoreham (Sussex) aerodrome, where we lived in Bungalow Town. We were supposed to undergo a course of instruction in flying antique aeroplanes rather like gigantic box-kites. I should have mentioned that previous to this we were supposed to have had a month's course in aeronautical engines, theory of flight, the Morse code, and the rigging and maintenance of aeroplanes, all of which, except the Morse, were absolute mysteries to me. I went first to Reading, where the R.F.C. had taken possession of the University Hostels, and part of the tramway depot. A week was more or less wasted here, waiting to join a class; and I was suddenly shifted at a moment's notice to a similar school at Oxford, living in Exeter College for about three days or so. With equal suddenness I was one morning transferred to Shoreham, without having had any of this necessary instruction.

The R.F.C. pilot officer who was to teach

me to fly these comic antiquities could handle
them himself all right, but was not gifted as
a teacher, and I was told to take one of the
lumbering old under-engined kites into the
air without having really felt the controls.
Ignorance being bliss, I had a go at it, managed to clear the sheds, and found myself
about 300 feet above the sea, slowly but
steadily leaving Old England behind. I tried
to turn, but only succeeded in side-slipping a
little nearer to the water. However, eventually I managed to make a very flat turn by
flying round in an immense arc, and, coming
over the sheds again, shut off and prepared
to land. As I did not flatten out properly I
broke one of the undercarriage struts, and
alighted in a somewhat ignominious fashion,
but I was really rather relieved to get down
at all.

After that I had two more hours' instruction, and really took control, henceforward
having no further trouble, and making several
solo flights without mishap.

October (undated).

Transferred, again at a moment's notice,
to Dover; still without any 'general' instruc-

tion. Norah and I found lodgings at St. Margaret's-at-Cliffe, and I used to go to the aerodrome each morning on a cycle (push).

Here we are on Service machines, and have to learn all over again; but I, at all events, have no trouble, for the instructors are all first-class. I begin to realize the real romance of flying here, in this cloudy gusty October weather, over the seashore and cliffs and the sprawling town and castled heights of Dover, over the green fields and purplish-brown woods of Kent.

We fly Avros, beautiful machines, but they are fitted with an 80-h.p. Gnome rotary engine, which has a terrifying habit of blowing out an inlet valve, and, if you are not quick at switching off ignition and petrol, of catching fire. We fly also steady old B.E. 2 C's, and B.E. 12's, on which last I went to 10,000 feet for the first time the other day, landing from that altitude with the engine cut off, a sensation I enjoyed.

November 10th.

Today I was given the right to wear 'wings' as a certified pilot, seconded from the regiment to the R.F.C., and granted a week's leave, long-looked for!

I never had any theoretical course, but was sent up for examination at Oxford all the same, before being given my wings. By cramming from other fellows' notebooks I managed to pass all right.

While stationed here I attended an investiture at Buckingham Palace to be given my M.C. You line up in order of seniority in an ante-room, and a sort of hook is stuck in the breast of your tunic. The King shakes hands and hangs the decoration on the hook. He looked and probably felt tired by the time he came to my turn, but he asked me if my wounds had healed. When you come out an attendant removes the cross and puts it in a neat case for you, and you walk out into the courtyard.

I have had no leave and very little free time during training, so Norah and I are greatly looking forward to a week together in Brighton.

November 12th.

After breakfast I went for a short stroll along the front, and on my return found Norah with an anxious, unhappy face, feverishly packing. She showed me a telegram.

'Why have you not reported to Adastral House as per my telegram,' etc. Of course I had never had their miserable telegram, but I rushed up to London, and submitted to the abuse of some arrogant young swine in an office, who when at length my explanation was given him, remarked, 'Well, your train to France goes at 11 tomorrow morning, and you still have time to catch it,' and dismissed me by picking up his newspaper again.

I did hope for a home station for a few weeks, in order to get a little more flying practice, as I have done only 23 hours' flying time, which seems little enough before going over Hunland. Also I had a lingering hope that I might get out to Egypt or somewhere in the East, being sick to death of the French and Belgian front. Often at night I think of Hill 60, and those trenches at Loos, and have to get a grip on myself to put it out of my mind.

I went back to Brighton, and broke the news to Norah casually, trying not to show how I felt, for it must be worse for a woman. A man has no time to think when he has to get on with a job, especially when he is with a lot of good fellows; but a woman is in

suspense all the time, especially so when she is
going to become a mother.

November 13th.

I am in France again, after a swift journey
over, a cold and somewhat rough passage.
The escorting destroyer kept plunging
through the seas and getting smothered with
spray. The Frenchmen on the train chat-
tered all the way, and the British sat silent;
they were going to their country, we were
leaving ours.

As I half expected, when I got here, there
was no hurry whatever! We are told we shall
probably be here several days.

November 19th.

The train from Boulogne was supposed to
start at 9, but did not arrive till midnight. I
spent the intervening hours in the Officers'
Club, running out now and again to see if the
train was in. When it came it was very
crowded, full of French civilians, terrible fug.
It was more than usually slow, so that by the
time we arrived at Abbeville, where I had to
change, I had fallen into a doze, and awaked
at Longpré, a dozen miles beyond, at 6 a.m,

I tumbled out into the snow, shared a fire with a soldier on duty, and obtained a few buns and some tepid coffee at about 9 o'clock. At 10 my train back turned up, and at noon I found myself at Abbeville. Having registered my luggage at Boulogne I found it at Abbeville all right. It was raining now, and my train to Frévent was due.

I dared not leave the station, as the train might leave at any minute, but at a quarter to three I chanced it, and went to the hotel opposite, to have my first meal since 6.30 the previous evening; omelette, ham, and cheese. I just got back to the station in time to catch the train, and jogged along in the dark for a long time. I shared the compartment with a French officer, a captain who was French A.P.M. at Armentières. He told me that he had a wife and six children, the youngest now three years old, who were in Lille. Think of it—he in Armentières, they in Lille, opposite. The shells go to and fro, but if his family were dead, he could not be more cut off from them.

Even a French train, having all eternity before it, arrives in the end, and I reached Frévent at about 6 o'clock. I found the R.T.O. there a good fellow, and so while his clerks telephoned for a tender from the squadron for me, we found a café and had an excellent little dinner and a chat by his stove afterwards.

My tender came at 9.30 and so at 10.45 I reached the squadron at last (at Savy near Aubigny), very sleepy. They gave me a drink and got me a bed, so this morning I felt better.

I have a tiny hut made of canvas, stretched on a wooden frame, which by now is looking fairly comfortable. I have bought a piece of matting, a chair, and so on, and in a few days my servant and I will make it quite snug, and (I hope) will cope with the draught. The mess is of course a camp one, but very good, considering. Everything is a bit rough, but luxury compared with the infantry, because you are not always on the move. In the infantry, if you do get a good billet, you are always moved on, or shelled out!

We have B.E.2E machines. Weather beastly. Several of us went for a drive to a place about 30 miles away to inspect a special new Hun machine that had come down in our lines.

November 20*th*.

Today very windy; clouds too low for any real work; but in the morning I thought I would like to take my machine up just to get to know her and my mechanics. I flipped about for half an hour; but not longer, as it was very cloudy, and a very high wind was blowing. I like my bus and feel quite at home. Fortunately the landing was a good one; I say fortunately, because half the squadron 'happened' to be watching. So I feel that I have 'taken my ticket', as they say. This afternoon I had a fresh breezy walk along lanes and over fields.

A stove will shortly be issued—I hope it comes soon. There is an issue of soft leather leggings, which come up to the thighs, and snow-boots to wear over them.

November 21*st*.

Wintry mist; no flying; mighty cold, especially in my little hut. I could not wait for the stove, so bought a Primus. It gives out quite a good heat, and I shall make a proper stove by putting it in an empty oil drum. So perhaps I shan't quite freeze tonight. Oh, I am glad I am not in the trenches this weather

—it would be like that 1914–15 winter over again.

November 27th.

Our C.O. returned from leave today. He is very popular, and I don't wonder. He is a master at Eton in private life, and a rowing Blue.

There is nothing doing yet. This morning I went up with an observer, to get the lie of the land, and the look of the country. Very cloudy. I was very confused by the masses of trench lines. They all show up white against the dark ground, and seem a perfect maze. No doubt one gets used to it, but today I could not make out one trench system from another, nor tell which was roughly our line and which the enemy's. Nor could I pick up any landmarks. The drifting masses of greyish white cloud kept obscuring the view, and I was altogether very muddled, and almost lost my way coming home.

Am reading 'Snow upon the Desert', by Miss Macnaughten, rather a jolly tale. Very good concert party here tonight, from the Canadian Corps.

Captain Guy Thrupp, an Englishman, is

our Flight Commander. He seems a stout
fellow, rather quiet, tall, rather good-looking.
Then there is Roger Dupré, tallish, loose-
limbed, fair wavy hair and a fair moustache,
and an agreeable smile; a loyal Canadian,
though speaking English with a French
accent. His father was a Frenchman, but he
comes from Saskatchewan. There is also in
the flight (B flight) one MacPhee, half French
and half Scottish, and in temperament more
the former; Duncombe is an average Englishman whom I knew at Dover; and Saltash, a
very tall fair West Hartlepool man, who is
known as 'Golly', from the way his light hair
sticks up. He has a sun-burned pleasant face.
A good companion, except when his liver
troubles him.

November 27th.

Last night a most luxurious hot bath in the
hut; boiled two gallons of water in a petrol
can on my stove.

This morning the squadron attempted a
bombing raid. Reached the prearranged
height over the aerodrome, and moved off, our
escort of fighting F.E.'s above us. But before
I had got anything like my height, one of

my cylinders blew right out. I had to descend quickly, so did not help to harry the Hun on this occasion.

Successful show—no casualties.

November 28th.

I have a paraffin lamp for light in the hut; and the Primus for heat, within an oil drum and a grating for asbestos bricks. Am having a small writing-table made by the carpenter. I have two large shelves, a horn window neatly draped by my servant with muslin, a coat-hanger made of a bent twig and a boot-lace, coconut-fibre matting, a stout chair, and a table covered with American cloth, which serves as a washstand. Above it a ledge for toilet articles; strung between two nails as a towel-horse; petrol cans containing water beneath the washstand; and a mirror that folds up.

Another bomb raid this morning. We got our height at dawn, and when our leader (whose machine is marked by streamers) fired a Verey light as a signal we assumed formation and set out. But the show was a washout. Stretching out over Hunland, like hundreds of square miles of soft snow away below and beyond us, was a vast sea of white cloud. We streamed over some distance, with our escort of F.E.'s above us, but there was obviously no break in the cloud bank, so back home we came.

Later on I went up to test an engine and nearly got lost in a fog.

November 30th.

Have had a special map-carrier made for my machine, and a mirror so that I can see behind me. Cold wintry mist over everything. I generally manage a short walk every day for exercise. I often go out with Dupré, or an observer named Gourlay, who won the V.C. in the infantry. We have a very nice crowd in our mess. The C.O. sets a good tone.

December 4th.

Gourlay and I went on a tender to St. Pol, and did, or tried to do, a little Christmas shopping.

Another bombing raid today, but again I was unlucky, as my engine would not give its revs, and I could not get the height.

December 5th.

Have discarded the oil drum (in my stove) and simply pile asbestos bricks on the ring of the Primus.

The mess has been adorned by eight large water-colours done by the C.O., also a frieze representing one side of the river at Windsor, and on the other the great bridges at Berwick-on-Tweed. The water-colours represent aerial subjects; B.E.'s and Nieuports with clouds all round, and puffs of Archie bursting, and France and the lines far below. Some fine atmospheric effects, especially one of the Evening Patrol. Quite a change from the usual Kirschner drawings of thin, pale females.

December 6th.

Bad flying weather again today, quite hopeless. We are not quite idle, of course; we potter about our machines, attend lectures, go for walks, and so on. I took my bus up this afternoon, but only for about 5 minutes, as there was a high rough wind and mist at about 700 feet.

Read two books lately, one in French called 'L'Éveil' and another by Una Silberrad called 'John Bolsover'. We buy odd books in the

o

village and pass them on when we have read
them.

Have obtained some canvas from the store,
and am having the annexe of my hut, where
my washstand is, curtained off; gives me more
warmth.

December 8th.

The mess has been further enriched by a
frieze done in body water-colour upon brown
paper by the Major, depicting a scene near
the Aisne in 1914.

December 11th.

Had a little adventure today. I took up
an observer (a very good fellow named
Duckett) for a practice artillery shoot over
the aerodrome, the weather being a little
better. After we had finished I steered west
while I wound in my aerial, and ran into very
thick cloud, and foolishly got lost. I had to
come down very low to get below the clouds,
and after flying round for a while I saw a very
large stubble field, so decided to come down
and inquire my exact whereabouts, as the
weather was so thick. I got down all right,
but when running along the ground I got

into a small hole I could not see, and then
bounced on to a large rut. The wheels
stuck in the soft soil, and the poor old bus
slowly tilted on to her nose and broke her
prop. My observer and I got hold of some
men and a rope, threw a couple of nooses
round the tail, which was sticking up straight
into the air, pegged her down, left a guard,
and 'phoned from the village near by for
assistance from the Squadron. Meanwhile
we were entertained to lunch by an R.E.
officer.

December 16th.

Wireless is wonderful. You just press a
key in your machine, and instantly the
battery has heard you, given the signal to fire,
and you see the flash of the guns far below.
Then you swing the machine round and
begin to fly towards the target, counting the
seconds and staring at, say, the four little
blurs on the landscape that are the enemy
gun-pits, your target. As you get over the
trenches a ball of black smoke appears and
uncoils, and another and another, perhaps
some distance below or above, perhaps un-
pleasantly near, followed by the cough of the

explosions, and occasionally, if the shooting is good, by the whizz of the shrapnel. You twist and dip and dodge, keeping your eye on the target, till you see a tiny black spurt of smoke and earth 200 yards over or short on to one side. You hastily pin-point the burst on your map, swing round again, and fly back to your battery, working out the correction as you go. Then when you are near enough you signal the location of the burst. You fly in a sort of elongated figure of 8, signalling the correction followed by the order to fire as you approach the battery, and then turning to observe. You must always direct the machine towards the receiver of the message, or the wireless won't carry.

If, however, you begin to make too regular a figure of 8 as you fly, Archie (the anti-aircraft gunner) gets to know just where you are going and will put his shrapnel right in your path. So the idea is to baffle him and turn unexpectedly in the other direction, or lose or gain a little height. Dodging Archie is quite a game and adds to the excitement of a shoot. You shout with delight when you have outwitted him and his bursts go wide,

but now and again he guesses right, and you
sail almost through his smoke, while all your
sinews tighten. Direct hits by Archie are,
however, very rare, and it is only quite seldom
that you get fragments through your wings.

Corrections are given by a clock code.
You draw concentric circles round the target
on your map of 25, 50, 100, 200, 300 yards
radius, and each ring is lettered. You also
describe, in imagination, corresponding rings
on the ground, and so a burst may be seen
on the C ring at 6 o'clock and is signalled as
C 6. By this the battery commander knows
he is on the line, but is so many hundred
yards out. Twelve o'clock is north.

Our own anti-aircraft bursts are a great
help and warning to us. Our bursts are
white, in contrast to the enemy's black, so
that if you see white puffs of smoke appearing
you know there is a Hun scout about, and you
turn for the safety of your own side of the
lines, signalling 'Wait HA' (hostile aircraft)
to your battery. The Hun scouts are much
faster than our 'Art-Obs' buses; even so, our
job isn't to seek a scrap, but to observe for
the battery below.

December 17th.

Cold, damp, thick fog. A 5-mile run with Duckett. I find that strenuous physical exercise helps to keep me from brooding. Norah continues to write cheerful letters, dear child.

December 18th.

Saw a tank for the first time, or rather several tanks. Flew over a tankodrome near St. Pol and had a good look.

Had some successful shooting with a Lewis gun and a revolver at tins in a quarry.

December 19th.

Exceedingly cold, and snow has fallen. I have taken to chewing gum in the air only (not too nice a habit elsewhere). It keeps the throat moist, and I think it tends to prevent the temporary deafness one sometimes gets.

Went for a long run this afternoon; tonight I am 'lazing' in front of a fire with a pipe, a book, and two or three friends.

December 21st.

Tremendous gale of wind and rain. Went

for a run for an hour, and felt extraordinarily exhilarated.

December 23rd.

All pilots of under two months' service in France have to pass a rather stiff exam, and we are in the thick of it now. Passed everything so far, and the worst is over.

It is wonderful to see the way they deal with the aerial photographs. They produce a dry print, enlarged to whatever size is required, from any plate, including removal from the camera, in half an hour!

The plate is removed from the slide, developed, washed for ten minutes, and dried by immersion in methylated spirit. The plate is then placed in a large acetylene lantern. In front is a board on which the paper is clipped. There is a cap of yellow glass on the lens of the lantern. The lens is adjusted and focused according to the size of the print required, and the cap is removed for exposure. The print is developed, bathed in hypo, washed for ten minutes, and dried in a few seconds. They do this by dipping it in methylated spirit, setting the whole thing alight, and blowing the flame out. This dries the print and puts a gloss on it. The print has been enlarged to the same scale as the large-scale map, and is then 'placed'.

December 24th.

I shall be getting up very early tomorrow morning, for the C.O. is taking me in the squadron car to the Somme, and if I am lucky I may see the regiment. We shall not stay long, as he wants the driver to get back in time for the Christmas dinner we officers are standing the men. I don't suppose there will be any church, as the padre who was occasionally seen round here, and who was, to tell the truth, a dull dog, has gone sick. It will be a long drive tomorrow, about 50 miles each way, but it is a good Crossley car, and we shall slip along.

I was not on any definite duty today, but I had a most enjoyable hour's flight. I had a fat observer wedged in the front seat with the guns. The engine was going splendidly, while the machine was perfect.

December 25th.

Rose at 5.30 this morning, had a hasty breakfast and set off with the C.O. and

'Bruin' for the Somme. 'Bruin' is a tall, big
fellow, rather jolly, with a fresh colour, and
brown moustache. We sped along in the
car, and reached the Divisional H.Q. we were
bound for in about two and a half hours,
rather farther than I thought. 'Bruin' also
wanted to see someone on the staff of my old
division, so we stayed, while the Major went
to the village farther on to find his brother.
I found that the regiment was farther up the
line, and that they were in billets; huts of
some sort; about an hour's walk away. I had
not time to go so far. After all, it was only
just a chance. They are coming out into
rest in a week's time, so I might get a chance
to see them then.

The Divisional H.Q. is in Fricourt, a
village which used to be within the Hun lines,
but which is now many miles this side.
Absolutely not a trace of this quite big village
is left, not one brick upon another. What
the guns spared, and that was little enough,
has gone to strengthen the roads, and now
you would never know that houses, inns,
shops and church had ever stood there.

Standing on a little eminence I could see
for some miles over this great battle-field.

Truly the painter of this war must be a land-scape painter. As far as you could see were rolling hills and valleys, brown earth pitted with upturned chalk, and battered filled-in trenches in places just discernible. Thousands of men were living in that space before me, hardly any were visible. Shelters were every-where dotted about in groups, bell tents, canvas huts, wooden shacks, iron huts; but no guns, for even the heavy guns were in advance of this place. Straight-flung wisps of smoke streamed out into the wind from the encamp-ments; now and then could be heard the distant menacing growl of high explosive; a few blighted trees straggled along the far sky-line. Overhead was a low purple sky, angry and threatening, with straight shafts of light darting downwards from the cloud. In spite of the human dwellings everywhere visible, the utter desolation of the country was sharply felt. At night this would not be so notice-able, for all this country is ablaze with light. Think of that, you people at home, who dare not pull up a blind without risk of punishment. Nobody bothers about lights in France, even close to the front line, nor ever has done. Near at hand a few moving figures were to be seen, a mounted man on the glistening road, the horse slowly lifting its feet from the slimy mud; and a few melancholy-looking mud-splashed big-boned Persian mules.

Tonight we had our Christmas dinner; some immense turkeys from Norfolk, Christmas puddings, of course, dessert, and drinks and smokes of various kinds. I drank, silently, to Norah.

The weather was very dull, showery, with very violent winds, so we did no work.

December 26th.

The weather is pretty awful again; fog first, now rain, so I did not fly. This morning I was practising with a revolver, and hit a 3-inch ring at 40 yards with the second shot; between me, myself, and the proverbial gatepost, I am rather pleased about this, as I have not had much practice. Just tired myself comfortably by a run before tea; while this evening after dinner we watched a boxing contest in one of the hangars.

December 27th.

For a change we had a glorious warm sunny day, though it is freezing hard tonight.

My afternoon walk was really delightful, it was a joy to be out.

I had a very peaceful job this morning. My duty was to fly a machine out to another aerodrome, and bring back one in its place. I found the way by the map, and thoroughly enjoyed the trip.

Reading this diary one would think the R.F.C. a very slack lot, who do remarkably little work. At this time of the year a corps squadron like ours, which specializes in such things as artillery work and photography, does have a fairly easy time. We are especially slack, because for the last two months we have been a sort of reserve squadron, just helping the others. We shall be busier before so very long, if all the rumours are correct.

The old Hun is said to be building a great line, with a maze of trenches protected by immense belts of wire, and ferro-concrete machine-gun blockhouses every fifty yards or so, from Arras down beyond St. Quentin. It looks as though we shall be here for years and years.

December 28th.

The weather is very cold, and my Primus

is not satisfactory. Even when it is going well, it does not make a canvas hut really warm, so I do not sit in my hut these evenings. If I get tired of the mess, I sit in a room in a farm across the road, which is Dupré's billet, which he shares with a Flight Commander of Scottish ancestry who in private life is a K.C. in Brisbane, lean-faced and lawyer-like, an amateur musician and full of humour. They keep a good fire, and always make me welcome.

However, it is rather rotten having the place so cold, and therefore the man with whom I share the hut (at present we have a curtain partition) bought today a little coal stove, so that we shall be able to get a good fug up. It has cost us about 12s. 6d. each, and is well worth it.

The fellows in this mess have come from all the ends of the earth, Australians, Canadians, Anglo-Indians, English, Scots, Irish, Welsh, rolling stones, and mixtures such as Anglo-Canadian-French, Anglo-Dutch-Canadian, Franco-Scot; and all sorts of professions, lawyers, clerks, schoolmasters, engineers, managers, musicians, and even soldiers.

Dupré, whose English is idiomatic yet broken, and his friend the Brisbane lawyer,

I have already mentioned; also Saltash, an
immense fellow, who generally lives in
Sweden, Finland, or Russia, among the
pilots. The star turn among the observers is
our V.C., a Stonyhurst and Sandhurst man
with a large broken nose. He is a devout
Roman Catholic, always ready for a rough
house, and apparently does not know what
fear is.

December 29th.

Today was held the last of the series of
examinations, and I have passed them all and
got them over.

Mild, but terribly wet. This squadron is
a 'happy ship' as they say in the Navy.

December 30th.

After dinner last night I went across to
Dupré's billet. We had a big red fire, comfortable chairs, chocolate, fruit and tobacco,
and books. I sang songs, which the Brisbane
lawyer accompanied on his banjo, so we three
had a cheery evening.

This afternoon I went in a tender with
two others to Arras, an ancient city close to
the firing-line. It is almost empty of civilians,

and has been badly battered by shell-fire, especially in the centre of the town, where the Cathedral and the Hôtel de Ville are completely in ruins. This great square is an extraordinary sight, piled high with rubble of brick and stone, and here and there crypts and underground passages have been laid bare. The savage bark of the guns echoes round the deserted ruins and the scarred and shattered houses, but otherwise a strange silence prevails. Only the twittering of a few sparrows round the crumbling remnant of a tower, or the squeak and scamper of rats can be heard.

I went to see two fellows in the 5th Battalion of the regiment whom I know. They were in billets in the town. It was my first visit to the place, though I fly over it nearly every day.

My room-mate and I have been busy this evening over the hut. We have installed the stove, with a chimney, and have completely altered the place. We have a fire burning now, which is a cheerful sight.

We have an organist of one of the cathedrals at home in our mess, a pilot; a good-hearted fellow, but quick-tempered and eccentric, and I'm afraid he gets his leg pulled a lot.

December 31*st.*

Weather very dud, nothing doing, might as well be at home.

After breakfast I spread myself out in front of our new open fire in the hut, and read pretty steadily on to about 3 in the afternoon—E. V. Lucas's new book. Before tea Thrupp, van B. and I went for a run, and this with a hot bath and tea to follow has made me feel very pleased with life.

Had a letter from Arthur, who is adjutant to the 2nd Battalion in Salonica. They have had one good scrap, in which the battalion did well—but generally speaking it is a quiet life. He adds, 'We don't see as many shells in a month here as come over in half a day in France. One can walk about anywhere by day without fear of being strafed. In fact I have ridden round the trenches.'

Had some whisky punch in the mess at midnight, with fireworks and 'Auld Lang Syne', seeing 1916 out and the New Year in. Couldn't help thinking of all the faces which are gone; and whether my turn will come this year; for as I write in this diary it is 1917.

1917

P

1917

January 1*st*.

WE have been further improving our hut with some dark blue hangings and curtains. It's a most comfortable and cheerful little room.

I was up for a short time today, testing another fellow's bus, but the engine was missing very badly, so I had to come down hastily.

January 4*th*.

An appalling morning, furious rain; but after lunch it quickly cleared up. I dashed for my bus, and tried to do a shoot, but there was a ground haze, and I could not pick up the target, so after flying about the lines for a while I came home.

January 5*th*.

Spent a full busy care-free day. Morning broke cloudy but fairly fine. I was down to do a shoot on some German positions with an observer. We had studied our maps well the previous night, so after testing our wireless and Lewis guns we were ready to start. We were able to get to a good height, and were not bothered by Archie, who only fired a few salvos (nowhere near us), probably owing to the fact that the clouds which sometimes hindered our observation also hindered his.

We were up about two hours, made our report, and were home in good time for lunch. At 1 o'clock I started off to see the regiment, which I had heard had come out of the line. It was a long drive, 60 miles at least, probably more, but I arrived at Battalion H.Q. by teatime. The C.O. was on leave, but I knew the acting C.O. well, and Cuming-Seton the adjutant, the doctor, quartermaster, and transport officer, so had a good time. Afterwards I went to see the officers and men of my old company. There have been many changes, but happily I found several familiar faces, and felt very much at home.

We drove home in bright moonlight. We were only just clear of Amiens when the Hun started to bomb it.

January 5th.

I have been married just a year today.

January 6th.

I flew some way behind the Hun lines this morning, and threw overboard a number of pamphlets written in German—propaganda, I suppose.

January 9th.

Poisonous weather again yesterday and to-day. I was up for a few minutes testing an engine—quite enough.

General Trenchard, the G.O.C. of the Flying Corps in France, inspected us today, otherwise there was nothing doing.

A fellow on a Nieuport Scout did a wonderful stunt for him to witness, rolling over and over sideways in the air. The pilot found out how to do it the other day by accident.

January 10th.

Have just returned from an entertainment given by the 42nd Casualty Clearing Station (R.A.M.C.) who live in these parts. It lasted about three hours, but surprisingly was not a moment too long. Absolutely first-rate and very funny; a running series of sketches and song scenas, splendidly rehearsed, dressed, staged and lighted. We often have travelling entertainments and cinema shows, for we have a capital little theatre in a big marquee, with a stock of scenes painted by our industrious C.O.

Had a short flip today, but nothing much doing. Part of the afternoon I finished a water-colour sketch of a Nieuport Scout landing on the aerodrome.

Dupré and I had a long walk and tea at Aubigny.

The mess has decided to hire a piano from Paris, and I have been detailed to make the arrangements.

January 11*th.*

Been snowing a good deal today, though it is not settling much. I was flying morning and afternoon between the snowfalls, and it was extraordinary to see the ploughed fields all white, in rectangles and triangles like a cubist picture, for the grassland did not hold the snow at all.

Amused myself today by writing parodies on five songs from Shakespeare, topical ones,

chiefly about people in the mess; and illus-
trating each with thumb-nail sketches and
caricatures. They caused a good deal of
merriment.

January 12th.

An excellent concert today; one of Lena
Ashwell's Concert Parties.

January 13th.

The Canadian Divisional Brass Band has
been putting up a heavy barrage this evening
in the theatre tent.

January 14th.

Thrupp, Duckett, and I went for a run,
splashing along the muddy roads. That's
all I've done today, except that I went up to
test the air, and found the clouds practically
sitting on the tree-tops.

Micky the magpie is our squadron pet.
He comes into the mess sometimes for a game,
and thoroughly loves a rough-and-tumble
romp. You can never catch him though,
however quick you are, even with his wings
clipped. He hops into the huts, head on one
side, and if you are not very careful he will

be away with anything bright. As soon as it is light you can hear him whistling and croaking and chattering, and he will run along beside you down the path. He quite enjoys being chivvied if caught thieving or trespassing.

January 16th.

Grey misty weather, with a hard frost. Spent some time walking in iron-bound roads and frozen fields.

January 18th.

Beaucoup snow.

January 21st.

Another day of east wind and hard frost, the snow still lying thick everywhere. Had nearly three hours' flying today. We have had a very slack time lately owing to the terrible weather and bad visibility. With an observer I was patrolling our section of the front for two hours this morning, most boring, just flying up and down, to and fro. Every day and all day the bit of line our squadron is responsible for is supposed to be patrolled, but at this time of the year it is not often possible to do it. I had to fly at 2,000 feet

today, couldn't get higher. Seems to me
rather a waste of time and petrol, though
after our forced inactivity even a dull job like
this has its points. But we are not fighting
machines, and are not supposed to go out
looking for trouble, while contrary to most
people's notions, an airman may fly all day
above the line and see not a sign of any life
or movement. All you can see is a wilderness
of pock-marked earth seamed with a maze
of chalk lines which are the trench systems.
Very, very rarely by a fluke you may spot an
enemy battery firing, and now and again
you may see a plume of smoke from a railway
train away in the back area. The patrol
could be done far more effectively by a Kite
Balloon with two or three observers using
field-glasses. Of course they would be farther
back, but they would be able really to watch
something closely instead of racing up and
down at 70 miles an hour.

I think the value of aerial reconnaisance is
overrated. Definite jobs of work such as
artillery shoots or photography are of course
most important, but I do not see much use
in this desultory patrolling. But perhaps
there is some obscure reason for it.

After lunch, while I was in my hut, a Hun machine came over quite low, going west. I dashed out, got the observer, and went up after him. Seven other machines went up as well. I never saw one of them, nor the Hun either, though I cruised about for nearly an hour. The weather was very thick. As a matter of fact, he landed about three miles away, having run out of petrol, and, I suppose, lost his way in the mist. We had the Hun observer in here to tea; quite a decent little chap.

January 22nd.

Flying today for some time, acting as escort to Thrupp, who was taking trench photographs. Another fall of snow.

January 23rd.

A piano has at last arrived in the mess. Very busy today; till now (9.15 p.m.) except for lunch and dinner I haven't had a moment. I have been up three times, and have also had a long drive to see the battery I have been spotting for. Weather glorious, though extraordinarily cold; snow everywhere. We shall get some real work done if it continues like this.

January 24th.

Very busy again at counter-battery work, and a visit to the battery afterwards. Perfect weather, cloudless sky, bright sun, and gleaming snow.

January 25th.

Thirty-three degrees of frost last night. A fellow in the artillery came to dinner. He brought some pipes, and after dinner he played 'Donuil Dhu', a strathspey, a pibroch called 'My Home', the 'Glendrewel Highlanders', and a reel. Late, after I had gone to bed and was asleep, a gang of fellows who were keeping it up came round to my hut, opened the door, and he played 'Donuil Dhu' again, while I sat up in bed. We had a haggis at dinner.

Busy again; $3\frac{3}{4}$ hours in the air in one go. Did a successful shoot with a heavy battery, registering their shots on two German batteries. It was the most successful shoot on our front since the squadron took over. To-morrow one of the Hun batteries is going to be thoroughly strafed, and I am going up to watch it. Being well registered they should not want much checking or correction.

This work is most interesting, and highly important. I really enjoy it.

January 27th.

Quite a good day. Went up solo at about 10.30 a.m. with a camera, and climbed to 10,000 feet. I then dropped over the lines to take photographs of the Hun battery positions we strafed yesterday. The wind was very strong, due east at about 50 m.p.h. I was unmolested, except for a little Archie.

After lunch I had no further duties, and as the weather was settled, I proposed to Gourlay, our V.C. observer, that we should go down to the Somme. He was quite keen, so at 1 o'clock we started off. Just as we were leaving the ground, letters from home were handed to us, and as soon as we were well in the air I read them. Two fine letters from Norah, and one from mother.

It was rather interesting finding one's way over strange country, and I was pleased when I sighted the leaning Virgin of Albert gleaming in the sun. I landed at Baisieux aerodrome, and soon found the battalion. We had taken about 50 minutes over the journey, flying across wind sideways, steering south-east to go south, thus allowing for drift.

Had about two hours with the regiment, returning to the aerodrome at 4. It was so cold that the engine wouldn't start, and we had to dope her thoroughly and swing her a lot; didn't get away till 4.30, arriving home at nightfall.

January 28th.

The weather has been so much better that I have averaged two hours a day war flying this last week. This is nothing very much, but a lot compared to what we have been doing.

My observer and I got rather fed up today, as we could not get our battery on to the target, so just as it was getting dark we dived on to the Hun trenches and let off our guns to ease our feelings.

January 29th.

On patrol today. Have left the squadron this afternoon and am living with a 6-inch howitzer battery for a few days to see the war. Billets in a cellar in St. Nicolas, near Arras. Am sleeping in the cellar, but the mess is a draughty room after the old style. Battery a jolly fine crowd.

January 30th.

An interesting day with the battery, seeing what an aeroplane shoot is like from the battery's point of view. A store of old Madeira has been discovered hidden behind some bricks in the cellar. Most useful.

January 31st.

This morning my observer and I went up to the battery's observation post in a support trench, where we watched the fire on the Hun trenches. The Major of another battery near by rang us up and invited us to lunch. We accepted, and while going round his guns one of our 'planes rang up from overhead and he took on a shoot with it. Of course we stayed to watch it through, and very interesting it was.

This liaison idea between the R.F.C. and the gunners is very sound. We get to know each other's point of view, and can thresh out difficulties.

February 2nd.

Returned to the squadron.

February 3rd.

Registered a big gun, and was pestered with the same old Archie in the same old way.

February 4th.

Bought a proper mattress; very necessary this bitter weather. More patrols, more registration. Two V.C.'s in our mess now.

February 6th.

Archie fairly riddled my bus today; she is docked for repairs. He is seldom so successful. Accidentally dropped N.'s letter in the mud this evening. Felt quite anguished.

February 9th.

A tremendous east wind, 55 miles an hour at 3,000 feet. Made work very difficult. You are either sitting almost motionless and a first-rate target for Archie, or tearing westwards much too fast, and having to struggle very slowly back. Up for over 3 hours, and after a hurried lunch dashed off again in a car with the C.O. to artillery H.Q. and two batteries.

February 10*th*.

We find the snow very difficult for observation; although the weather is remarkably
clear up above, the bursts often show up
badly or not at all against the white, and also
it is trying to the eyes to stare on to snow for
hours at a time day after day. There is
generally a mist on the ground, but from
3,000 feet upwards all appears clear, for one
can see through the ground-haze. As a
matter of fact, it has suddenly clouded over
tonight, and is warmer, so it may thaw.

George Bernard Shaw turned up here the
other day, but I was out and didn't see him.
I suppose the C.O. looked after him, but
nobody else seems to have taken much notice.
He is just a name to most of them, and, anyhow, only another civilian sightseer.

February 11*th*.

Slack day for me; too cloudy to see the
target this morning. This afternoon the
squadron struck a bad patch. Two fast Hun
scouts dived out of the clouds on to one of our
machines doing a shoot, and brought it down
in Hunland, both pilot and observer being
killed. We are rather sad about it, for we

were such a happy family, and these things never cease to be a slight shock.

The same two Huns attacked another two of our machines shortly afterwards. One dived on the tail of one of ours and shot it about a lot, luckily missing the occupants, but they were almost done for when one of our scouts sailed up, dived on the Hun in the nick of time, and brought him down in flames, thus avenging one and saving another. We also had an air mechanic gunner observer wounded in the leg by a lump of Archie.

February 12th.

There was an unusual quietness in the mess last night, for the two that went west were very popular. Tonight the C.O. stood champagne for dinner, and we had a hectic evening.

Have been very successful lately with my shoots, and am getting the important jobs. Very glad; perhaps they will keep me on artillery work, and off the photography jobs, which are pretty deadly in these old B.E. machines.

February 13th.

The adjutant, I notice, is detailing me for the easy safe jobs this week, no doubt because

I am due for leave. Just had a hot bath, and am sitting in pyjamas by the fire, while Fitz prepares hot cocoa and jam roll.

February 21st–March 6th.

Fortnight's Home Leave. No time or inclination to write in my Diary.

March 7th.

Back at the squadron. A stiff wind and a choppy sea crossing. Travelled on the Staff train from Charing Cross by looking as haughty as possible and by walking through without showing my ticket. I had said my good-byes at home, for I can't bear these leave-takings at the station. To anyone it must be a poignant sight; hundreds of brave women, who keep back somehow their tears, and turn sadly and empty away when the last lingering look has been taken at the vanishing train.

March 8th.

A biting north-easter, with intermittent rain and snow.

March 9th.

More snow. Early patrol; uneventful. Recommended for promotion to full lieu-tenant in the R.F.C.

March 11*th.*

Had a bit of excitement today. I was up in the air on a shoot with a heavy battery. I was doing the shoot myself, my observer acting as gunner. We had been up the best part of three hours, and I had got the battery well ranged on the target. I had given the signal 'battery fire', and I was watching and correcting the salvoes, when suddenly I heard pop-pop-pop-pop-pop-pop behind me and bullets began to swish by our heads. Tears appeared in the fabric of the wings and a landing wire parted. It appears that one or more (my observer said three) of Richthofen's Circus—the Hun 'planes are painted with all sorts of gaudy stripes and patterns and devices—had got on our tail, but luckily missed with their first bursts. My observer, who had apparently been half asleep instead of keeping a look-out, leapt up and began firing over my head; while I put the machine into a steep spiral instantly, in order to throw out the aim of the enemy, about the only possible manœuvre with an antiquated B.E. bus. It would have been hopeless to attempt to out-fight or out-manœuvre. While we were whirling round and round, my

observer kept pumping away with his Lewis
gun, and when he had fired all his rounds the
damned idiot dropped his gun almost on my
head. I dodged and took it on my shoulder.
He just threw up his hands in despair. I
straightened out for a moment, and handed
him a spare drum, which he put on the gun,
and stared wildly round the sky. I bawled
'Is he gone?' He nodded in reply. A
merciful deliverance; if he or they had per-
sisted they must have got us. My observer
swore he hit one machine, and it may be so,
otherwise I cannot see why they did not
finish us off.

The next thing was to discover where we
were. I made out we were nearly over Lens,
miles over the trenches, about 1,000 feet up.
Our troubles were not over, as we had to
struggle back, but we were unmolested except
for a little rifle-fire from the trenches.

The machine was not seriously shot up,
but I found a bullet in my seat, which had
struck something hard and was all twisted up.

A scrap is the normal day's work of a
fighting machine, but a poor old B.E. feels
very injured if it gets caught. We had a
lucky escape. It is true B.E.'s have been

known to bring down Huns by a lucky shot,
and I fancy we must have hit ours.

March 13th.

It is a little after nine. I am sitting on my
bed, by the fire, with the two oil lamps lit.
F. is on leave, but Roger has dropped in, and
is sprawling on the other bed reading a novel.
There is very little wind, and that south, and
not a sound but the running of the motor
that drives the electric light dynamo, the
faint crackle of the fire, and an occasional
footstep past the door. And I am thinking
of things that one should not think of if one
is to give all one's powers to the job in hand.
Enough.

March 14th.

General Trenchard paid us a visit this
afternoon, and remained to tea. Pouring
with rain, and so no work today. I went for
a long run across country, but it was mech-
anical. Why am I running? I asked myself,
and stopped; then I ran as fast as I could back
to the aerodrome.

March 15th.

Visibility too bad for work. Dined with the Kite Balloon section. It is marvellous to watch the stream of heavy traffic on the Arras road. Limber and lorry, guns, bombs, small-arm ammunition, tools, rations, and shells, shells, shells, an everlasting stream. They are making a colossal dump at Achicourt.

March 16th.

Events are moving fast; things are becoming electric and absorbing. It has been plain to us for some time that a big offensive is boiling up in these parts from the intense counter-battery work we have been doing; and the news is we are to shoot soon on second-line wire, with big stuff, 8-inch and nine-two howitzers on belts of wire! The P.B.I. are 'for it' before long. Thank God I'm not with them!

March 17th.

Remarkably bright and clear, though very windy. Did some useful registration on patrol. Saw four poor devils going down in flames.

March 18th.

A successful shoot, and tea with the battery afterwards. Another day nearer the Big Push, which everyone is discussing.

March 19th.

Perfectly awful night, a westerly gale quite 70 miles an hour, and blinding rain. How ghastly it must be for the men out feeling for the Hun, with not even a trench to crouch in! I was up on patrol this morning—a rough passage, as the clouds were very low, and the wind strong and gusty.

After lunch I went for a walk with Saltash, returning just before the rain came.

The other day, Dalny, our observer from the West Indies, did a pretty good piece of work. His pilot (the man who was half a Frenchman) was shot and killed by a Hun. As the machine was falling out of control, D. climbed out of his seat, got on to the wing, sat on the dead pilot's knee with one leg hanging out, and though he could not reach the rudder, landed the machine undamaged behind our trenches. He is only an observer on probation, very young and inexperienced. Wonderful luck, of course, but what nerve and pluck! He had fought the Hun with his machine-gun and beaten him off. I envy him, for in the mess he laughs and jokes, and doesn't seem to care a damn; while I find myself flying, in imagination, with a Hun on my tail. I wish they'd scrap all the B.E.'s.

March 21*st*.

More bad weather. Cold and gusty, with snowstorms all day long, and wonderful clouds in the sky, great towering mountains of cloud. You sail in between the marvellous cloud-precipices, or round the topmost pinnacles into the serene blue above, or dodge away from the angry threatening black wall that is a snowstorm. Given the right day, flying is an exalting experience, and one longs to have someone to share the beauty and the wonder of it. With the roar of the engine filling one's ears, one swings along, the aeroplane responsive to the lightest touch of foot and hand, thousands of feet in the air, with the dazzling blue dome of the sky above, and the great cloud mountains below and around you. Solid earth is far below, seamed with white tree-bordered ribbons of roads, and where the fields are, chequered with rectangular strips of colour of the various crops or fallow land, plough, or pasture. Early in the morning the hollows are filled with blue shadow, or creeping wraiths of mist, rivers flash in the sun or reflect a steely gleam, as the racing cloud-shadows darken the scene.

Facing you is a great white mass of cloud. With a rush it seems to come at you, and in a moment you are enveloped in a dark and dank clinging mist. The aeroplane bucks and kicks, while you keep your eyes on your compass and pitot [1] tube, for if you do not fly well and truly by them, you may come out in a vertical dive or upside down; there is nothing else to guide you. Suddenly it gets lighter, the mists fling away, and you are out, between blue sky and coloured earth once more.

Our flight commander and his observer have been shot down over the lines, but their machine is reported to have descended more or less in control, so there is a chance that one or both are prisoners and not dead.

Reading my entry of the 19th, I find I haven't conveyed the exact situation. It is only when I'm not flying that I dread it;

[1] Air speed indicator.

when I'm in the air, I don't care a damn,
but enjoy it.

March 23rd.

Am now sharing a hut with Saltash.

The old Hun has gone back miles on the
Somme, leaving us all the mud and ruins, and
settling safe in the Hindenburg Line. The
newspapers say it is a great victory for us.
Actually it seems a masterly move on his part,
for he has an immensely powerful system behind him.

March 24th.

Archie and the Huns have been busy today, and more of our squadron are gone.
However, chiefly by what is alleged to be the
better part of valour, I have got through
another day.

Roger is our flight commander now.

March 26th.

It appears that poor 'Bruin' and his observer
were struck by a direct hit from one of our
own heavy shells. I wonder it does not
happen more often. These last few days the
air has been full of shells, constantly the
machine leaps and bucks in the wind of one

as it goes by, and several times I have actually
seen the shell in flight. The heavy howitzers
shoot thousands of feet into the air on a long
range.

We gave them a military funeral. 'Bruin's'
father, a C. of E. padre, buried them. It was
pretty hard for him. The weather was bad,
so most of us were able to attend. The flag-
covered coffins rested in front of the altar in
the Corps Church in Aubigny, and on them
were polished shell-cases filled with flowers.
After the first part of the service we went to
the cemetery, where there was a large firing
party of air-mechanics, and some Hussar
trumpeters for the Last Post.

I wouldn't mind going west for myself,
but frankly I get quite sick when I think of
Norah.

March 28th.

A busy day; two flights, one of $1\frac{1}{2}$ hours
and the other of 3 hours, and hanging on to
telephones about the shoots most of the rest
of the day. My observer, Joe Darke, is a
cheery lad from Toronto, and we get on very
well. On the way back from the line we
always sing; he turns round in the front seat

and beats time to 'Jingle Johnny'. We
neither of us can hear, of course, but we keep
time with our lips, and his beat.

Years ago, I remember the regular Tommies
singing as they came out of action, after that
ghastly attack in Ploegsteert Wood. Then
I thought they were 'wonderful'. Nothing
wonderful about singing because sentence of
death is temporarily suspended.

March 29th.

All day long we are either in the air or on
the 'phone with the battery. The shelling
from our guns is intense, and growing every
day, the sky is full of whistling shells and
roaming aeroplanes. 'Hunland' is dotted
with leaping bursts: from in front of Vimy
Ridge to Bullecourt the German batteries are
being strafed, the front-line trenches are
beginning to look battered in places, and
away back volcanoes are erupting in the
zones of wire, that look like faint grey
smudges on the brown landscape. Zero day
must be fairly soon.

Saw several 'planes go down in flames near
the Hindenburg Line. Whether theirs or
ours I don't know.

March 30th.

We have just finished dinner, and are sitting in the hut. There is a blazing fire; behind the curtains a petrol can of water is heating on the Primus, for after a hot bath and some hot toddy I shall crawl luxuriously into bed. Saltash is busy preparing a shoot for tomorrow, sitting on his bed with his maps; Roger is sipping his grog and making out the flight orders; while I write this diary and a letter to Norah. I feel better today; I think it was my liver, not my nerves, thank goodness. *Labor omnia vincit.* I have been very busy indeed; over 5 hours actually in the air, and have been working in the office the rest of the time. Moreover, the clouds were at 2,000 feet, so we had to keep low, there was a very strong and gusty wind, the pockets made by the heavy artillery fire pitched us about, we were annoyed by Huns, and kept dodging the skirts of rainstorms; but Joe (my observer) did an excellent shoot on the first trip, and I managed a successful one on the second.

In the infantry, after a hard day's work one probably got little or no sleep at all, and at best could but bury one's dirty self in a filthy smelly dug-out, and pretend one liked the cold and damp; but in the R.F.C. one has the privilege of cleanliness, warmth and comfort after one's work is done. Having been so long an infantry man I can appreciate the R.F.C. Besides, one sees with one's own eyes the result of what one is doing. The P.B.I. are slaves, in effect.

March 31st.
Promotion to full lieutenant in R.F.C. is through.

April 1st, Sunday.
Am going to the Corps Church in Aubigny tonight.

April 2nd.
Today the clouds were higher. Up for 3 hours and strafed a Boche battery. The wind was so high that it was almost like being in a captive balloon; one was almost stationary (relative to the earth) if one put one's nose into the wind. These B.E.'s are hopelessly slow and dud; hearses, in fact.

Afterwards I just managed to make the aerodrome before a heavy snowstorm, which lasted for some hours. Landing in a 60-mile gale with sleet in your face is no joke.

The other day I saw four rooks flying in formation over Arras at 4,000 feet!

Strafing batteries today, and dropping bombs, and indulging in frightfulness generally. A dog-fight about a mile away this afternoon, scores of machines. Saw about a dozen go down, some in flames—don't know if they were our fellows, or Huns. Probably both.

April 5th.

Dreadful news from home; wife very ill and baby dead. Tormenting to think that at almost any other time but now I could get special leave. I am to have the first call in the Third Army.

April 6th.

Flying again. No news from N.

April 7th.

Still no news. Unbearable almost. This is X day.

April 8th.

Still very busy; plenty of flying. N. reported better, thank God. Y day. To-night a hell of a roar and a glare from Arras way. They say the Hun shelling blew up

the Achicourt dump. The sky is ruddy to
the zenith.

April 9th.

N. out of danger, and the show a great
success! My observer (Lloyd this time) and
I booked front seats at the matinée, and it
was the most astonishing sight I have ever seen
or ever shall see, I suppose. We were on the
lines at dawn while it was yet twilight, shortly
after the infantry had gained the front-line
trenches. The whole place was a mad pan-
demonium of flashes and bursts and lights and
smoke, and stupendous noise that even we
could hear above the roar of the engine.
Apart from the shell bumps, I suppose that
it was the most awful weather that anyone
could possibly fly in. We were pitched about
by the shells, there was quite a 50-mile an
hour gale blowing, and what was worst of
all, a blinding snowstorm nearly all the time,
and very low clouds.

Before I left the ground, the C.O. shook
hands and said, 'Take care of yourself.'
Not exactly what a Regular soldier would
say, perhaps—but there is no C.O. like ours!

Our job was to locate the active hostile

batteries, and to signal their position to our heavy guns. After flying for nearly an hour about a thousand feet or so up, we were hit by a large shell splinter in the petrol tank, a ground burst, I think. Vapour and petrol were pouring out, and as I feared fire I made for the ground, while Lloyd vainly tried to plug the hole with his map and gloves. We got clear of the main-trench system, found a patch of fairly unencumbered ground, and, dodging the shell-holes against the wind, landed successfully and undamaged close to the forward observation post of an Australian 9-inch battery whom we knew well. The F.O.O. gave us breakfast after we had 'phoned to the squadron.

The infantry are well away up the slope of Vimy, and the Welsh Harp has fallen. Our field guns are all going forward at the trot.

The ground was too bad and the space too small to get off again after replacing the petrol tank, so we rode home, and the machine is being dismantled and taken back by road. Luckily the Hun was too busy to shell the machine, and by the end of the morning he was not in a position to do so! With America in, the old Hun must feel his number's up!

R

April 10th.

Flying. Got under a dog fight, but fortunately kept clear in my old sluggard. Saw one of our single-seaters going down in a spin; it passed quite close to me. Its wings were all shot up, and the pilot was lolling as though unconscious. As it went down one wing crumpled back, and it crashed in flames. *Dulce et decorum. . . .*

April 11th.

The gunners have now had an opportunity of seeing some of the targets on which we have been ranging them during the period of preparation. Battery after battery has been knocked out and destroyed, and the wire in their second and third lines is blown to shreds, and partly buried in the chalky loam everywhere thrown up and re-thrown up by our bombardment.

Leave not through yet. N. signed a letter written by the nurse, with a shaky little cross. She tells me not to worry, the poor darling.

April 12th.

On patrol this morning, and after lunch drove to the Aircraft Depot at St. Omer to bring back a new machine. A very high wind. Flew low along the railway line in a storm of sleet. Journey took 50 minutes. Leave still not through.

April 13th.

Fetched another machine from St. Omer. Feeling fine today. It was grand to see the golden evening sun flashing on the sea.

Dropping my little bombs this morning, I had the lucky fluke of a direct hit on the railway bridge. Archie got very angry, but no real harm was done to us. Very thankful to get back to earth again. No leave yet.

April 14th.

The very high and gusty wind made flying tricky; just like managing a fractious restive horse. I was on patrol from 6 to 9, and then had a 100 miles cross-country trip to the Depot and back. C.O. awfully decent to me.

April 15th.

'Golly' Saltash is funny tonight. He wears a worried look, and is writing a prodigiously long letter, and tearing up as much as he writes. Of course it is to a girl. I rather gather he has put his foot in it somehow, from the growl he emitted about the unreasonableness of women. 'I cannot understand them at all,' he says. I tell him he never will quite, but that further experience will do wonders.

N. much better.

April 16th.

No sign of leave yet, but Norah progresses well.

I was up doing a shoot this afternoon. I had the luck to spot two new German batteries (which will receive attention) and strafed a third. The Major and several others were waiting for me, and they first cursed me for keeping them in suspense (for I had been a long time out) and then congratulated me. I have never seen the Major so pleased. It was such a rotten day that they expected me home early, but, as a matter of fact, now and again visibility was excellent.

I can't prevent myself from flying in imagination when I am in my hut at night, however much I try to force myself to read. Sometimes I imagine myself going down in flames, and how it would affect N.

April 17th.

Great gale of wind and rain last night, and a hangar blown down. No flying.

Heard a good story of a R.F.C. sentry who had orders to admit no one to an enclosure. A general came along and wanted to enter, and was refused. 'Confound it,' said the general, 'don't you see who I am? I'm the G.O.C.' 'Very sorry, sir,' said the sentry, 'couldn't do it, not if you was G.O.D.'

April 21st.

My leave came through just as I was putting on my leather coat. The Major himself came and told me. 'There's a tender waiting,' he said, 'off you go.' I felt quite shaky. He is an extraordinarily decent man.

I am writing this on the boat at Boulogne, just before we cast off for England.

May 3rd.

Patrol flight today, the first since my special leave. I think I shall 'get my flight' and promotion in the squadron very soon now, as Roger is going home for a spell shortly.

Another attack by the Fifth Army south

of Arras this morning. It failed. We don't seem able to get forward at all after the first successes on the 9th of last month.

Heard today that the French mutiny in the Champagne was on a very big scale; for once the rumours that constantly travel up and down the lines like 'wind up' appear to be correct. The staff-major who told us, in the mess, said that several divisions had actually set out to march to Paris. It seems incredible.

I have had a return of those beastly internal pains I had in the trenches near Colonne last year, going round the front line one night, when I almost fainted with the pain, and crept into the mess dugout, doubled up and done to the world. Next morning everything was normal. It will be pretty awful if it comes on suddenly in the air.[1]

May 4th.

Newman turned up unexpectedly from the regiment today. I gave him a joy-flip on my 'bus.

Later, patrolled. On the way home the

[1] It wasn't until eighteen months later that this was diagnosed as gallstones, and I was operated upon.

throttle connexion broke, but I managed to
land safely on the switch, after excessive
anxiety. Nowadays my heart leaps into my
mouth when the slightest thing goes wrong,
such as engine missing or otherwise dropping
a beat.

I can't help thinking about N. and the
child. They said it was such a pretty little
baby; but born too soon, too soon. A baby
would have been a comfort to her if I went
west. However, it's best forgotten, I suppose.

May 5th.

Patrol shoot today, with Joe as observer.
The best visibility this year. Between us we
got 3 batteries. Warm and languid in this
hut. Can hear a cuckoo calling steadily, and
distant stuttering bursts of 'lewie' gun practice
on the range.

May 6th.

Jerky, spidery writing is due to the fact
that I'm trying to write with my left hand,
in the Canadian Hospital at Doullens. I have
made a dog's dinner of my 'bus, and someone
else will probably get command of the flight.

A pretty sister has just drifted into the

ward. Asked her what telegram had been sent home. 'Well,' says she, 'they said you'd broken your nose only, for they didn't know about your collar-bone then.'

'Broken my nose? I've broken my nose? What on earth is the matter with everyone? There's nothing the matter with my nose. Can't I take off this absurd plaster?'

'No, of course you can't. The doctor said you'd broken your nose, so I guess you must have.'

I tweaked my own nose vigorously, and then pulled it hard. She looked rather shocked, then spoke to me soothingly, and tried to persuade me to get some sleep. 'You'll feel better when you've had some sleep,' she kept repeating, and deliberately refrained from looking at my nose. I asked her if I could write for a bit longer, and she readily agreed.

However, my collar-bone is broken all right. My right arm is strapped tight to my body, and yards and yards of sticky plaster are wound round it. I suppose they had a little bit left over, and wishing to comply with the official demands for economy, stuck it on my nose.

May 7th.

The Canadian doctor must have been a vet. He treats one as if one were a horse. However, I count myself fortunate, for he has not definitely ordered the sticking plaster to be stuck on my nose again.

The sisters here are dears.

May 8th.

The day before yesterday I had a day off; hence my mummy-like state in this place. What happened was this:—

I thought I would flip over to see Stannard, who was a pilot with me at Dover and is now at the depôt at Candas, a few miles away from the aerodrome. After flying in that direction for some while I saw below me what I took for hangars, with men standing about near them. Thinking this was Candas, I put her nose down, and, after making a good landing, taxi'd towards the hangars. To my surprise the men started running towards me—scores and scores of them. A bit queer, I thought, as I switched off. They flocked round the 'bus in such excitement that it began to rock. I asked them if this was the depôt, and about a dozen voices began to talk at once; however,

I learned that the depôt was about a mile
away. I looked where they pointed, and saw
the hangars.

'All right, thanks, I see, I see', I kept
repeating. 'Now please keep clear of the
machine', as I got out to swing the prop.

The engine started at once, and I climbed
into the cockpit again. About fifty men
were now around the 'bus, holding the struts,
and generally getting in the way. They were
trying to be helpful, of course, but actually
they were hindering. I shouted to them to
stand clear, but they did not understand; I
shouted again, and waved them away, but
they stuck there, while others came running
up. Suddenly the greatest rage rose in me,
and I began to curse and swear at them without control. The congestion loosened a
little, but still they remained. I opened the
throttle full blast, the grass was flattened
under and behind the fuselage; caps were
flung off heads, and I saw many duck or
throw themselves down as the 'bus began to
bound over the field across the wind. I felt
a violent blow on my shoulder as the earth
tilted and seemed to hit me after a crack and a
crash; and the machine was flying to splinters

in a sunken lane that I saw vividly as it faded out with all sensation of falling. Then I was lying on the grass, just by the edge of the road, seeing faces above me anxiously looking down, and hearing a murmur of voices that sounded near, and yet remotely connected to my lying on my back. I remember feeling very much ashamed that I had cursed them, a thing I don't think I've done before; but thank heaven I had enough wits left to say that I was sorry.

'That's all right, sir,' they replied cheerfully; and then my stretcher was sliding into the iron grooves of an ambulance, and I remember cheerful faces massed at the back of the car. Afterwards I must have slept, for I remember nothing until I found myself, with a curiously thick and obstructed nose, lying in bed in this cool and airy ward.

May 11th.

My birthday.

One of the sisters comes from London, Ont., and thinks London, Eng., must be 'a poor sort of burg'. They call me 'Old Scout'. This afternoon they took me down to their sitting-room, cretonne curtains and cushions, and a real civilized tea, bless them.

May 12th.

> '*We're going home, we're going home,*
> *The ship is at the shore,*
> *And you must pack your haversack,*
> *For we won't come back no more!*'

I begged to be allowed to stay at the Canadian Hospital, and return to the squadron, but the doctors were firm (thank God!). I don't want to go with part of me, but most of me *longs* to go. I am so damned tired, yet contented, and every throb of this hospital ship's propeller takes me nearer England, and home.

EPIGRAPH

[WITH the exception of half a page written on the day the Armistice was signed, my War Diary ends here. A brief account of my doings up to November 1918 may be of interest. I was sent home for a long rest, and in November 1917 resumed flying at Winchester, as instructor to observers. There I remained until the end of the war.

During the last few months of 1918 we had thousands and thousands of Americans in and through Winchester. The infantry used to come into Liverpool, down by train to Winchester, and thence to Southampton. Many of them had to march all the way from Winchester to Southampton at one time on account of a railway strike, and I felt rather ashamed of this welcome. Their physique was magnificent, the pick of a great nation.

I was promoted Captain and Flight Commander at the school. My Flight consisted of a Flight-Sergeant (fitter), an excellent rigger, a cabinet-maker by trade, and up to all the faking tricks of the antique trade; one or two air mechanics; a few W.R.A.F.'s; and a 'bunch' of Americans.

I am afraid it sounds discourteous, but the women were not of much use in the aerodrome. I kept one as a clerk, and there was really nothing else that women could do in a flight, except to clean wires.

The Americans were all big fellows, chafing with impatience at being kept in England. They wanted to 'share in the fun over there'. They were all supposed to be fitters (no riggers), but they didn't know the first thing about engines, and our sweating and over-worked flight-sergeant had to try and teach them. The trouble appeared to be that they had been units in production factories, accustomed to do one specialized job only. To please them, and keep them keen and in temper, we took each man up for a joy ride. They felt they were in the war, then.

One day came a knock at my office door, and an immense American in blue overalls entered.

'Say, Captain,' he said, with an awkward salute, 'can I speak to you for a minute?'

'Certainly.   What is it?'

'Waal, Captain, I joined the Army to fight the Heinies, not to sit around here filling your flying arks with gasoline and treacle. I want you to arrange for me to see a few Heinies while there are still any left.   I promised my girl a hair out of the Kaiser's whiskers.'

All I could say was that I would mention his request to go overseas to his own officer, but that I had no power at all with details of the American Expeditionary Force. He sighed, stared at his boots, saluted in a dejected afterthought, and went out.

As I recall it now, ten years afterwards, he seems to express the spirit of all the men in the war, before they got to the real thing.

All that summer I did my flying in leather cap and goggles, a khaki drill jacket and shorts, brown stockings and shoes. Sometimes I longed poignantly to be back with my old comrades in the regiment, or in the squadron (but nearly all were gone by the time the Hindenburg Line was broken in October 1918); and at other times dread and

terror would break into my rest at night. All
men who went through the war will understand this.

Here is the last entry in my Diary proper,
and so my book ends.]

November 11*th*, 1918.

Thank God the end of the awful blind
waste and brutality of war has come, and
let us pray it may never return. Man prays
to God, because he feels instinctively there
is a Power outside himself, yet the answer to
such prayer depends on man himself. After
this lesson, is man too little-minded and for-
getful to banish the things that cause war?

I am feeling rather ill and depressed, in
spite of all the rejoicing around me; immea-
surably relieved, glad to be alive, and glad
we have won, but tired and a little sad.

Lightning Source UK Ltd.
Milton Keynes UK
UKOW03f1049191014

240296UK00001B/215/A